Bourton

Gillingham

Motcombe

Kington Magna

SHAFTESBURY

Stour Provost

Cann

Todber

Woodyates

Marnhull

Margaret Marsh

East Orchard • Compton Abbas

albridge

West Orchard • Fontmell Magna

Ashmore

Handley

Pentridge

Hinton
St Mary

Manston • Sutton Waldron

Farnham

Newton

Hammoon • Iwerne Minster

Chettle

Cranborne

dlinch

Shillingstone • Iwerne Courtney • Tarrant Gunville

Wimborne
• St Giles

Alderholt

Fifehead Neville

Steepleton

Tarrant • Hinton

Gussage
St Michael

Edmunsham

Oakford
Fitzpaine

Hanford

Tarrant
Launceston • Long •

Gussage All

zelbury

Stourpaine • Pimperne

Crichel

More
• Crichel

Woodlands

ryan • Ibberton

Durweston

Tarrant
Rushton

Horton

Stoke Wake • Woolland • Turnworth

Bryanston • Blandford
Forum

Witchampton

Hilton

Winterborne
• Stickland

Blandford
St Mary • Tarrant Keynston

Chalbury

Holt

as

Winterborne
• Clenston

Tarrant Crawford

nghams •
Melcombe • Milton Abbas

Spettisbury
Shapwick

Colehill

e • Cheselbourne

Winterborne
Whitchurch

Sturminster • Pamphill •
Marshall

WIMBORNE
MINSTER

Hampreston

Dewlish

Winterborne
Kingston

Anderson

Corfe
• Mullen

Canford
Magna

West
• Parley

Puddletown

Bere
Regis • Bloxworth • Morden

Winterborne Tomson

• Lytchett Matravers

Tolpuddle

urleston Turners Puddle

Athelhampton

Lytchett Minster

POOLE

R • Woodsford

Hamworthy

ne Came • Moreton

st Knighton

East Stoke

Arne

Brownsea Island

dmayne

WAREHAM

Newton

• Owermoigne

Wool

Winfrith Newburgh

xwell

Combe Keynes

Chaldon
Herring

East Lulworth

Studland

gton

West
• Lulworth

Steeple •

Corfe Castle

Church Knowle

Tyneham • Kimmeridge

Swanage

Worth
Matravers

CHANNEL

THE MAKING OF THE ENGLISH LANDSCAPE
Edited by W. G. Hoskins

Dorset

by

CHRISTOPHER TAYLOR

HODDER AND STOUGHTON

To
my wife

Preface

THE MAIN PROBLEM of writing a book on the Dorset landscape is twofold. First, there are such great variations in the geography of the county that any generalisations about the history of the landscape will usually be wrong. More important, one is quite overwhelmed by the amount of material available to the landscape historian.

The county will shortly possess a detailed survey of all existing buildings and earthworks before 1850, by the Royal Commission on Historical Monuments (England), which will give it an advantage over all other counties for many years to come. It also has two useful volumes of the Victoria County Histories of England. There is an incomparable series of the *Proceedings of the Dorset Natural History and Archaeological Society*, and of the *Somerset and Dorset Notes and Queries*, both packed with information. The County possesses an excellent Record Office containing large numbers of useful documents, and a County Museum which has a large collection of transcriptions of Public Record Office documents, as well as an immense wealth of books and papers. There is also a good early county history by J. Hutchins.

The labour of sifting all this material and relating it to the varied landscape of Dorset has been greatly eased by a number of organisations and individuals. My greatest debt is to the Royal Commission on Historical Monuments. Not only have the Commissioners, through their Secretary Mr A. R. Dufty, allowed me access to much of their, as yet, unpublished material, but it was the Commission which gave me the opportunity to work in Dorset for seven extremely happy years. During these years I was to come to know the county in a way that happens to few. In addition, in that time, I was privileged to work under and with a group of the finest landscape historians and field archaeologists in this country. To all the Salisbury office Investigators past and present go my sincere thanks for everything that they taught me.

I would also like to thank Mr R. Parsons for assistance over many of the illustrations. To my colleague Mr D. J. Bonney special thanks are due. His great knowledge of topographical history unstintingly shared with me over many years enabled me to formulate some of the ideas in this work. I am also grateful to the Dorset Natural History and Archaeological Society, who through the good offices of their Secretary Mr R. Peers, have given me an immense amount of help.

Finally, my thanks go to the editor of this series, Professor W. G. Hoskins, whose wisdom and kindness have not only made the writing of this book much easier than I anticipated but I believe made it much better than it would otherwise have been.

C. C. TAYLOR

Whittlesford,
 Cambridgeshire.

Contents

List of Plates

ACKNOWLEDGMENTS

The author wishes to thank the following for permission to use their photographs:
J. Allan Cash: Plates 1, 2, 6, 29, 31
The Royal Commission on Historical Monuments (England): Plates 3, 9, 10, 15, 16, 18, 19, 21, 22, 25, 30, 32, 33, 34, 38 (Crown Copyright Reserved)
The Committee for Aerial Photography, Cambridge: Plates 4, 5, 8, 11, 13, 17, 37 (photographs by J. K. St. Joseph, Cambridge University Collection: copyright reserved)
A. F. Kersting: Plate 7
The Ministry of Defence (Air Force Department): Plates 12, 14, 20, 26, 35 (Crown Copyright Reserved)
The National Monuments Record: Plate 24
Plate 23 is taken from John Kip's *Britannia Illustrated* (1709–16); and Plates 28, 36 and 39 from J. Hutchins, *History of Dorset,* 3rd edition (1867).

List of maps and plans

Editor's Introduction

SOME SIXTEEN YEARS ago I wrote: "Despite the multitude of books about English landscape and scenery, and the flood of topographical books in general, there is not one book which deals with the historical evolution of the landscape as we know it. At the most we may be told that the English landscape is the man-made creation of the seventeenth and eighteenth centuries, which is not even a quarter-truth, for it refers only to country houses and their parks and to the parliamentary enclosures that gave us a good deal of our modern pattern of fields, hedges, and by-roads. It ignores the fact that more than a half of England never underwent this kind of enclosure, but evolved in an entirely different way, and that in some regions the landscape had been virtually completed by the eve of the Black Death. No book exists to describe the manner in which the various landscapes of this country came to assume the shape and appearance they now have, why the hedgebanks and lanes of Devon should be so totally different from those of the Midlands, why there are so many ruined churches in Norfolk or so many lost villages in Lincolnshire, or what history lies behind the winding ditches of the Somerset marshlands, the remote granite farmsteads of Cornwall, and the lonely pastures of upland Northamptonshire.

"There are indeed some good books on the geology that lies behind the English landscape, and these represent perhaps the best kind of writing on the subject we have yet had, for they deal with facts and are not given to the sentimental and formless slush which afflicts so many books concerned only with superficial appearances. But the geologist, good though he may be, is concerned with only one aspect of the subject, and beyond a certain point he is obliged to leave the historian and geographer to continue and complete it. He explains to us the bones of the landscape, the fundamental structure that gives form and colour to the scene and produces a certain kind of topography and natural vegetation. But the flesh that covers the bones, and the details of the features, are the concern of the historical geographer, whose task it is to show how man has clothed the geological skeleton during the comparatively recent past—mostly within the last fifteen centuries, though in some regions much longer than this."

In 1955 I published *The Making of the English Landscape*. There I claimed that it was a pioneer study, and if only for that reason it could not supply the answer to every question. Four books, in a series published between 1954 and 1957, filled in more detail for the counties of Cornwall, Lancashire, Gloucestershire, and Leicestershire.

Much has been achieved since I wrote the words I have quoted. Landscape-history is now taught in some universities, and has been studied for many parts of England and Wales in university theses. Numerous articles have been writtten and a few books published, such as Alan Harris's *The Rural Landscape of the East Riding 1700-1850* (1961) and more recently Dorothy Sylvester's *The Rural Landscape of the Welsh Borderland* (1969).

Special mention should perhaps be made of a number of landscape-studies in the series of Occasional Papers published by the Department of English Local History at the University of Leicester. Above all in this series one might draw attention to *Laughton: a study in the Evolution of the Wealden Landscape* (1965) as a good example of a microscopic scrutiny of a single parish, and Margaret Spufford's *A Cambridgeshire Community* (*Chippenham*) published in the same year. Another masterly study of a single parish which should be cited particularly is Harry Thorpe's monograph entitled *The Lord and the Landscape*, dealing with the Warwickshire Parish of Wormleighton, which also appeared in 1965.[1] Geographers were quicker off the mark than historians in this new field, for it lies on the frontiers of both disciplines. And now botany has been recruited into the field, with the recent development of theories about the dating of hedges from an analysis of their vegetation.

But a vast amount still remains to be discovered about the man-made landscape. Some questions are answered, but new questions continually arise which can only be answered by a microscopic examination of small areas even within a county. My own perspective has enlarged greatly since I published my first book on the subject. I now believe that some features in our landscape today owe their origin to a much more distant past than I had formerly thought possible. I think it highly likely that in some favoured parts of England farming has gone on in an unbroken continuity since the Iron Age, perhaps even since the Bronze Age; and that many of our villages were first settled at the same time. In other words, that underneath our old villages, and underneath the older parts of these villages, there may well be evidence of habitation going back for some two or three thousand years. Conquests only meant in most places a change of landlord for better or for worse, but the farming life went on unbroken, for even conquerors would have starved without its continuous activity. We have so far failed to find this continuity of habitation because sites have been built upon over and over again and have never been wholly cleared and examined by trained archaeologists.

At the other end of the time-scale the field of industrial archaeology has come into being in the last few years, though I touched upon it years ago under the heading of Industrial Landscapes. Still, a vast amount more could now be said about this kind of landscape.

Purists might say that the county is not the proper unit

[1] *Transactions of the Birmingham Archaeological Society*, Vol. 80, 1965.

for the study of landscape-history. They would say perhaps that we ought to choose individual and unified regions for such an exercise; but since all counties, however small, contain a wonderful diversity of landscape, each with its own special history, we get, I am sure, a far more appealing book than if we adopted the geographical region as our basis.

The authors of these books are concerned with the ways in which men have cleared the natural woodlands, reclaimed marshland, fen, and moor, created fields out of a wilderness, made lanes, roads, and footpaths, laid out towns, built villages, hamlets, farmhouses and cottages, created country houses and their parks, dug mines and made canals and railways, in short with everything that has altered the natural landscape. One cannot understand the English landscape and enjoy it to the full, apprehend all its wonderful variety from region to region (often within the space of a few miles), without going back to the history that lies behind it. A commonplace ditch may be the thousand-year-old boundary of a royal manor; a certain hedge-bank may be even more ancient, the boundary of a Celtic estate; a certain deep and winding lane may be the work of twelfth-century peasants, some of whose names may be made known to us if we search diligently enough. To discover these things, we have to go to the documents that are the historians' raw material, and find out what happened to produce these results and when, and precisely how they came about.

But it is not only the documents that are the historian's guide. One cannot write books like these by reading someone else's books, or even by studying records in a muniment room. The English landscape itself, to those who know how to read it aright, is the richest historical record we possess. There are discoveries to be made in it for which no written documents exist, or have ever existed. To write the history of the English landscape requires a combination of documentary research and of fieldwork, of laborious scrambling on foot wherever the trail may lead. The result is a new kind of history which it is hoped will appeal to all those who like to travel intelligently, to get away from the guide-book show-pieces now and then, and to know the reasons behind what they are looking at. There is no part of England, however unpromising it may appear at first sight, that is not full of questions for those who have a sense of the past. So much of England is still unknown and unexplored. Fuller enjoined us nearly three centuries ago

"Know most of the rooms of thy native country
before thou goest over the threshold thereof.
Especially seeing England presents thee with
so many observables."

These books on The Making of the English Landscape are concerned with the observables of England, and the secret history that lies behind them.

Exeter, 1970   W. G. HOSKINS

1. Dorset before the Saxons

The natural landscape. The pre-Roman scene. Roman Dorset

The natural landscape

DORSET IS ON the whole a surprisingly little-known county. It is true that many thousands of people spend their holidays at the main resorts of Swanage and Weymouth and from them become acquainted with the wonderful coastline of south Dorset. Fewer, but still a considerable number, visit the well-known beauty spots such as the delightful village of Milton Abbas. But relatively few people penetrate other areas of Dorset in all their varied aspects. Even in this day of the ubiquitous motor-car there are still large parts of the county where even in the height of the summer season no visitors are seen. How many people have discovered the delights of the vale of Marshwood, north-west of Bridport, with its scatter of stone-built farms set in the wooded vale almost completely surrounded by high hills? Who have squeezed their cars along the narrow road up the chalk-cut valley of the river Hooke on an early summer morning and found Toller Porcorum with its delightful church emerging from the mists? Or climbed the slopes of Melbury Beacon and watched the storm-clouds race across the wooded Blackmoor Vale and burst open over the chalk heights of Hambledon Hill; or walked the wild open heaths of east Dorset on a winter's afternoon with flurries of snow lightening the scene?

It is the variety of landscape in Dorset which gives the county its great charm and which has resulted in the equally varied landscape history. Dorset has a greater variety of rock type and scenery than any other county in southern England. From the Isle of Purbeck in the south-east with its limestone plateau, clay vale and chalk ridge, one moves north-west across wide open heathlands which give way gradually to the rolling chalk downs which occupy most of the centre of the county. These in turn end dramatically along a high escarpment and are replaced by the clay vales, ribbed by low limestone hills to the north-west, and the more rugged sandstone and limestone heights and clay vales of west Dorset (Fig. 1).

Yet this basic fivefold geological division of the county and its bare description does nothing to make us appreciate the beauty therein. Nor does it help us to see how and why these different parts, assisted or held back each succeeding generation in their work of changing and shaping the landscape. It is far better to turn to the county's poets and writers to understand both these points, for as W. G. Hoskins has said "poets make the best topographers".

Thus William Barnes, Dorset's great rural poet, captured the essence of the chalk downs and their history when he wrote over a century ago:

> The zwellen downs, wi' chalky tracks
> A-climmen up their zunny backs,
> Do hide green meads an zedgy brooks,
> An' clumps o' trees wi' glossy rooks,
> An' hearty vo'k to laugh an' zing,
> An' parish-churches in a string,
> Wi' tow'rs o' merry bells to ring,
> An' white roads up athirt the hills.

Here, better than any geographer or historian could describe, is the real setting for man's activities in this part of the county for at least 200 generations. The deep, well-watered valleys, set among the rolling downs, were the primary areas for settlement at all periods of our history and controlled

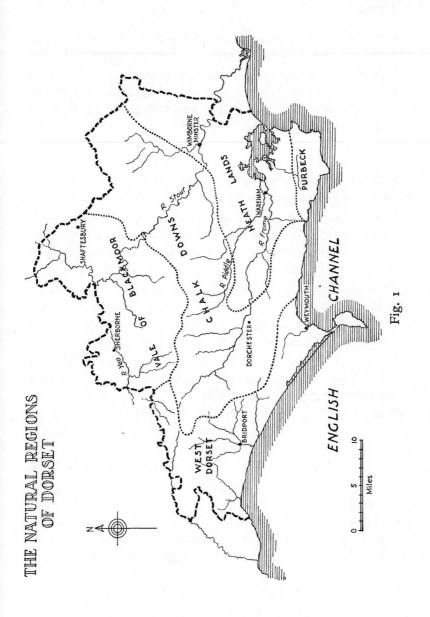

THE NATURAL REGIONS
OF DORSET

N

SHAFTESBURY

R. Stour

R. Yeo   SHERBORNE

VALE   OF   BLACKMOOR

WIMBORNE
MINSTER

CHALK   DOWNS

HEATH   LANDS

R. Piddle

R. Frome

WAREHAM

PURBECK

DORCHESTER

WEST
DORSET

BRIDPORT

WEYMOUTH

ENGLISH   CHANNEL

0   5   10
Miles

Fig. 1

the shape, size and development of these settlements. Similarly the downs themselves by their form, soils and aspect conditioned the type of agriculture, its distribution, expansion and contraction and indeed by their very nature have preserved for us today various kinds of farming activities which we can still see (Plate 1).

And Thomas Hardy described his Egdon Heath as "The untamable, Ishmaelitish thing that [it] now was it always had been. Civilisation was its enemy; and ever since the beginning of vegetation its soil had worn the same antique brown dress." This gives us the background to these wild, barren, infertile lands in which man throughout the ages has had to wage a ceaseless war against the ever encroaching bracken and gorse in order to keep it back from the poor fields wrested at great cost from the harsh environment.

In contrast, the well wooded north-west of the county, with its low hills and vales, and its plenteous streams, at first hindered and then helped man's conquest of the landscape. Its heavy clay soils held back the prehistoric farmers, but in later times it became a rich agricultural area, in which successive generations were able to establish new homes and fields continuously for nearly 2000 years regardless of conquerors, pestilence or economic decline. Hardy sums it all up as "the . . . undulations of the beautiful Vale of Blackmoor . . . in which the fields are never brown and the springs never dry."

For west Dorset we must turn back to Barnes where we find the best description of that land of broken hills and clay vales, where countless farmers slowly extended their fields out across the valleys and up the hillsides (Plate 2).

> Sweet Be'mi'ster, that bist a-bound
> By green an' woody hills all round,
> Wi' hedges, reachen up between
> A thousan' vields o' zummer green.

Plate 1 Cranborne Chase. The highest part of the chalk downs of Dorset which are everywhere dissected by deep narrow valleys. The fields on the ridge tops are of eighteenth- and nineteenth-century date.

Plate 2 The still wooded Marshwood Vale in the west of the county. Many of the fields extending up the hillsides were hacked out of the woodland far back in Saxon times.

Plate 3 Bronze Age barrow group, Winterborne Abbas. Here on relatively low-lying ground an accident of medieval tenurial history has preserved this remarkable prehistoric cemetery intact.

Plate 4 Hambledon Hill. Here a mighty Iron Age fortress crowns the hilltop. Top right, are the fields of Child Okeford enclosed piecemeal over many centuries from the former open arable strips.

Plate 5 Iron Age settlement and fields, Turnworth. A narrow track winds its way through the fields and passes the circular ditched feature which is the Iron Age farmstead. The fields themselves show traces of later temporary ploughing of medieval and eighteenth-century date.

Plate 6 Ashmore, the village pond. This pond probably dates from the Roman period at least and has enabled man to live on this exposed hilltop ever since.

So our county's writers give us the true background of the landscape and help us to appreciate its beauty and its history. Let us now look at both in more detail.

The pre-Roman scene

Most historians, even those alive to the history of the English landscape, tend to ignore or dismiss the part played in the making of that landscape by the prehistoric and Roman peoples of this country. In many counties, the part they played is perhaps negligible, or more likely obscured by later changes. Dorset, however, is one of a number of counties where the true importance of these people can be clearly seen if not fully understood.

Let us then look closely at the nature and use to be made of the available archaeological evidence, for it is of a very different order from that which most historians are used to working with. Dorset generally, and especially the chalk areas, is immensely rich in standing archaeological remains. Almost every ridge is dotted with Neolithic or Bronze Age burial mounds or barrows. Many of the prominent hilltops have formidable Iron Age fortresses on them, and there are many thousands of acres of prehistoric or Roman fields often with settlement sites in or around them. From our present-day villages and towns in the valleys, we tend to look towards the downlands and assume that because this is where most of the visible remains of the prehistoric and Roman past lie, their builders and occupiers lived only there and have no relationship to our present-day communities. Nothing could be further from the truth.

The archaeological sites exist on the high land *only* because later people have not used this land intensively and so it is in these areas that the remains have been well preserved. As we shall see there is evidence that both the prehistoric and Romano-British peoples lived in the valleys and low-lying areas of Dorset as well as, or even more than, on the high ground. Indeed it is probable that for much of the prehistoric and Roman periods the high hills and downland were marginal lands occupied and perhaps cultivated only under pressure of relative overpopulation. It is not going too far to say that with the exceptions of those parts with extremely heavy clay soils, such as the vales of Marshwood in the west and Blackmoor in the north-west, the prehistoric and Romano-British people lived in and worked on most of the land in the county. This is vital for understanding the history of the Dorset landscape, for it means that the Old English settlers, whose arrival to many people usually marks the start of the history of the man-made landscape, moved into a fully settled and largely tamed countryside with the marks of over 4000 years of man's activities stamped upon it.

The evidence for this overall occupation during the prehistoric and Roman periods is perhaps not convincing to the historian used to firm and often relatively complete documentary material. The different nature of archaeological evidence and its haphazard and slow collection results in its being ignored or misinterpreted by historians. But it can and must be used. It is evidence of great value to the landscape-historian.

Using both this archaeological evidence, and documentary historical evidence for the later periods, in this and the following two chapters, a picture of continuous development of settlement and land-use within the county, from the remote prehistoric past until at least the fourteenth century A.D. largely unaffected by race, political events and land tenure, will be advanced. In this way the process of the occupation, taming and filling up of the whole Dorset landscape will be seen.

The earliest people to have had any effect on the Dorset landscape as we see it today are those known to archaeologists as the Mesolithic hunters and fishers, who appear to have lived in the county between about 8000 B.C. and 3500 B.C. Their numbers must have been extremely small, and being apparently nomadic hunters and fishers their effect on the landscape was probably minimal. But they had fire, and axes capable of felling trees, and together these made it possible for them to have had a devastating influence on the natural vegetation of the wooded valleys where they appear to have lived and hunted. It is clear from the thirty-odd sites known to be associated with these people, that in the main they lived in the lower-lying areas. There is a marked concentration of sites in and around the heathlands, in the clay vale of the Isle of Purbeck, behind the Chesil Beach south-west of Weymouth and along the river Stour. Relatively few sites are recorded on high land.

These people were succeeded, well before 3000 B.C., by a larger and more advanced group of settlers arriving from the continent of Europe, probably via south-west England. These are known as the Neolithic peoples. Their appearance in the archaeological record is marked by the first occurrence of pottery, the bones of domesticated animals and evidence of farming and trade. Their effect on the Dorset landscape was due in the main to the fact that they were the first people whose basic way of life was mixed farming. There is growing evidence that they not only cultivated hand-dug plots, but perhaps even ploughed small fields and it is certain that much natural scrub and woodland was cleared by burning or cutting, particularly on forest margins. Likewise goats, sheep and cattle were kept in increasing numbers and would in turn have helped to reduce and alter the natural vegetation. The somewhat prosaic animal bones recorded on the sites of these people reflect the gradual extension of open ground and a reduction of woodland. It seems likely that between 3000 B.C. and 2000 B.C. the chalk downlands of the county gradually lost their light woodland cover and began to be covered by the expanses of turf which remained the basis of agriculture in these areas until the nineteenth century.

While the huge long barrows or burial mounds of these people and at least two of their hilltop meeting places on Hambledon Hill near Blandford Forum and at Maiden Castle near Dorchester, are familiar, their known settlement sites are as yet few. This is in part due to the fact that these people were semi-nomadic, but also because archaeologists have only recently started to look for them. However, it is important to note that of the four certain settlement sites unassociated with the temporary hilltop meeting places, three were in relatively low-lying areas. The site found near Wimborne Minster in 1962 was on a low spur projecting north on to the flood plain of the river Stour at only sixty feet above sea-level. Again the notable series of Neolithic finds from the area south-west of Sherborne, on the river gravels of the river Yeo, shows a habitation site in a similar position, and in this region particularly there are suggestions of further sites all along the Yeo valley. This indicates that the Neolithic peoples were living, for part of their lives at least, in the river valleys of the county, in a terrain very similar to their Mesolithic predecessors.

Around 2000 B.C. another group of settlers moved into the county, the first of the Bronze Age peoples. These quickly intermixed with the existing peoples largely because their way of life was virtually the same although in archaeological terms they were very different and certainly had a more advanced technology. So in terms of landscape history they continued the alteration of the natural vegetation that their predecessors had started. Though as yet none of their settlements is known anywhere, a clue to the whereabouts of these may be seen in the siting of the contemporary burial mounds of which many hundreds still survive. A very large proportion of these, though on high land, are not on the summits of hills but often on spurs or false crests overlooking valleys. They can be seen silhouetted against the sky-line from these valleys where perhaps their builders lived even though their position on the highland itself may be relatively inconspicuous. A good example of this may be seen in the area around Dorchester. On the great ridge, south of the town, are hundreds of burial mounds of the Bronze Age peoples and many are in a very inconspicuous position when viewed from close by. But viewed from below in the valleys of the rivers Frome and South Winterborne they stand out, and it is at Dorchester, on the edge of the river Frome, that the upstanding remains of two very large ritual sites or 'henges' of the early part of this period exist, Maumbury Rings and Mount Pleasant. The builders of these burial mounds are more likely to have lived in the valley of the Frome around their 'churches' than upon the windswept ridge. This was left to the dead to continue their watch over the living in the valley. In other places there is evidence that even the burial mounds were sited on relatively low ground (Plate 3).

In the three centuries before 1000 B.C., a further migration of people into Dorset took place, probably from across the Channel. They appear to have landed in the Bourne-mouth area and in time moved inland up the river Stour and across the downlands in the north-east and centre of the county. The lines of their advance are known only from their burial mounds and flat cemeteries but the concentration of these on the valley sides and heathland of south-east Dorset suggests that they were clearing and occupying land from which later peoples have removed all trace of their living sites. The remaining places where their fields, and the curious linear ditches which were probably the boundaries of 'ranches' for stock, still exist are now confined to the higher chalk downlands where later activity has never reached. But these people undoubtedly lived elsewhere and

if the general distribution of their burial sites is any indication they must have occupied large areas of low-lying parts
of the county, and almost certainly lived in permanent
settlements. Only one of these has been excavated and that
is on high chalk downland near Sydling St Nicholas, north-
west of Dorchester.[1] The site was a single farm consisting of
a small circular wooden hut and a circular barn or byre set
on one side of a small yard which was surrounded by fields
through which a track approached it. The fields were typical
of those in existence right through to the end of the Roman
period at least; small rectangular or square plots of an
acre or less bounded by banks or lynchets. This site is
significantly the earliest permanent settlement known in the
county lying on high ground and it may be that it represents
the extension of settlement from the more favourable lowland areas to the drier, less hospitable, uplands.

It has to be remembered that much of the lower land was
not unfavourable to prehistoric man even with his primitive
agricultural techniques. Apart from heavy clay land in
places such as the vales of Blackmoor and Marshwood,
Dorset has on the whole fairly light soils. This is particularly
true of the chalklands where the relatively sheltered valleys
would surely have been far more attractive than the adjacent
ridge-tops. The latter must have been permanently settled
only when the better land had been used up and the settlement at Sydling St Nicholas may reflect this relative over-
population.

To use one such site as evidence of overpopulation by
1000 B.C. would be extending even archaeological evidence
beyond its limits. However, there is support for such a
view from elsewhere. After 1000 B.C. the archaeological
record is marked by increasingly large numbers of weapons.
Swords and spears become common and these may be of
some importance from the point of view of landscape

[1] Rhatz, 'Excavations at Shearplace Hill', *Procs. Prehistoric Society,* 1962.

history. The appearance of such weapons suggests that intertribal warfare may have been taking place on an increasing scale probably as the result of an expanding population and the consequent need for more arable and grazing land. The countryside was filling up and more and more land was being cleared, settled, cultivated and grazed, to such an extent that some people were being forced to live permanently on high ground.

These indications of rising population are increased after 600 B.C. when, archaeologically, we move into the Iron Age. The most characteristic sites of this period are the hilltop fortresses, the so-called hill forts, of which there are some thirty in Dorset (Plate 4). They range in size from the huge and complex citadel of Maiden Castle near Dorchester, which with its massive fortifications and evidence of large-scale occupation comes near to being an Iron Age town, to the tiny fort of Spettisbury Rings near Blandford Forum which is unlikely to have enclosed much more than a single farmstead. These hilltop fortresses indicate the further development of organised warfare and the need for protection and suggest that an increasing population was the cause of it. The relatively large numbers of rural settlements of this period also indicate an increase in population, and excavations at a number of them give us an idea of the wide variation of types of settlement from single farmsteads to small villages (Plate 5).

The obvious inference to be made from the hill forts and the scattered hamlets and farmsteads lying on the high limestone hills and chalk downlands of the county is that it was in these areas that the Iron Age people lived. But again this inference is not entirely correct as a careful examination of *all* the available archaeological evidence shows. One can scarcely expect to find complete Iron Age settlements on the lower-lying lands of Dorset, as these have inevitably suffered destruction by later settlement and cultivation. But chance finds in sufficient quantities in these areas do show, not only that Iron Age people lived here, but indicate that perhaps more of them lived here than in the higher areas.

For example, in the area south-east of Blandford Forum, while there are a number of settlements of Iron Age date, together with the remains of contemporary fields on the downland on either side of the deep wide valley of the river Stour, there is also evidence for Iron Age occupation on the lower slopes of the valley along the edge of the flood plain. Similarly, further downstream near the Hampshire border, though the only major Iron Age monument is the hill fort of Dudsbury (itself on the very edge of the river), Iron Age finds in sufficient quantities to indicate settlements have been found in a number of places on the river terraces of the Stour in this region. Sites are known at Langham, near Hampreston, at Hampreston itself, and south of West Parley, all on the north side of the river; and at Sleight, Corfe Mullen, south of the river, while more exist further east in the Hampshire part of the valley. Nor should it be thought that evidence of lowland Iron Age occupation is confined to the major valleys of Dorset. In the clay vale of Blackmoor, on the same limestone ridge that was subsequently occupied in the Roman and later periods, Iron Age occupation has been found at Marnhull. In west Dorset recent archaeological work has indicated Iron Age settlement in the deep upper valley of the river Brit near Beaminster as well as at its mouth at West Bay, Bridport. Finally, in Purbeck, where a considerable amount of archaeological work has been carried on, exactly half of all the known Iron Age sites lie either in the deep central clay valley or in the low-lying seaward areas below the limestone plateau.

It is fairly clear that by the beginning of our era the landscape of Dorset was relatively well filled with people living on and cultivating both the highlands and the lowlands of the county, and so organised that they controlled and depended on clearly defined areas of land or economic units over which they exercised a jealous guard.

Two points must be emphasised. First, many lowland parts had been occupied continuously for many centuries. Secondly, what permanent settlement there was on the highland was considerably less than perhaps we have often been led to believe and appears to be due to relative over-population and a consequent expansion of settlement from the lowlands on to marginal land.

Roman Dorset

The remarkable physical remains which mark the Roman period, such as the amphitheatre and aqueduct of the Roman town of Dorchester, the massive aggers or raised cause-ways of some of the Roman roads and the fine mosaic floors of many of the villas, tend to overshadow the more impor-tant effects of the Roman period which, though more diffi-cult to discern, are vital in understanding the pattern of the modern landscape.

Perhaps the most important effect of the coming of the Romans on the Dorset landscape was the four centuries of peace which they imposed on the warring Celtic peoples who occupied the county. This resulted in the acceleration of population growth, which we have already noted with the attendant increase in the numbers of settlements and the extension of agricultural land. This is clear from the archaeo-logical record. The numbers of known occupation sites of the Roman period run into hundreds and they are to be found in almost every part of the county.

Yet the picture is not one of sudden change followed by a static period. Changes can be seen occurring during the whole four centuries of Roman rule. At the moment our view is still somewhat blurred in detail but the main outlines are fairly clear. For the first five generations of

c

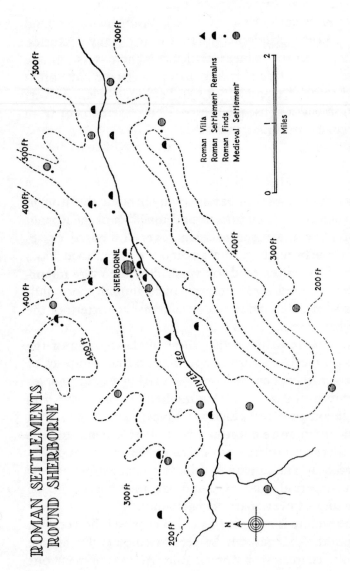

ROMAN SETTLEMENTS ROUND SHERBORNE

300 Ft
300 Ft
300 Ft
300 Ft
400 Ft
400 Ft
400 Ft
400 Ft
200 Ft
300 Ft
200 Ft
300 Ft
400 Ft
300 Ft
200 Ft

SHERBORNE

RIVER YEO

N

▲ Roman Villa
◖ Roman Settlement Remains
• Roman Finds
⬤ Medieval Settlement

0   1   2
Miles

Fig. 2. The area was clearly intensively occupied during the Roman period and almost certainly more settlements of this time still remain to be discovered. The importance of Sherborne itself during this period is also significant in view of its subsequent development as a Saxon religious centre in the eighth century.

Roman rule there is evidence that many Iron Age settlements continued to be occupied and also that new ones came into existence. Some of these new ones do lie on the high chalk and limestone parts, but the great majority appear in the lower areas. Detailed work in the Sherborne area, in the valley of the river Yeo, has produced over a dozen Roman occupation sites (Fig. 2), some showing evidence of earlier Iron Age occupation. Similar work in the Isle of Purbeck has resulted in the discovery of nearly fifty Roman sites, many with Iron Age antecedents. Most of these early settlements appear to be rather squalid dwellings, usually single farmsteads or small hamlets, completely in the Iron Age tradition of living conditions. Three examples will show this. At one of the high downland settlements, at Woodcutts near Handley in north Dorset, there was little evidence of Roman civilisation. It was apparently first occupied just prior to the Roman conquest as a single farmstead and remained little changed until its abandonment around A.D. 370. Throughout this long period the peasant farmers continued to live in a succession of wooden huts with little except pottery to distinguish their material way of life from that of their ancestors. Likewise at Iwerne Minster, on the edge of the vale of Blackmoor, excavation has shown that a similar farmstead existed from the late Iron Age to the end of the second century A.D. At Studland on the southern edge of the south Dorset heathland, circular huts of a very primitive nature and completely in the Iron Age tradition formed part of a hamlet in existence for the first fifty years of Roman rule.

From the second century and throughout the third and fourth centuries changes are discernible. Large numbers of lowland and valley settlements came into existence but, as far as the rather meagre records show, far fewer new settlements appeared on the higher parts. Further, while the upland settlements usually remain as primitive farmsteads as at Woodcutts, many of the lowland settlements were radically improved in material terms. Thus at the Iwerne Minster site the early crude wooden huts were replaced around A.D. 300 by a simple rectangular structure of flint rubble. Though still somewhat rustic, it certainly had some pretensions to be civilised and one of the living rooms had painted wall plaster. At Studland, the circular huts were abandoned in the early second century and a group of rectangular cottages constructed. In general many of the new lowland settlements seemed to reflect a great increase in wealth and civilisation, and villas such as the one at Maiden Newton near Dorchester in the valley of the river Frome and that at Hinton St Mary on the low limestone ridge within the Blackmoor Vale, are notable for their high level of Roman material culture. So there are definite indications that the richer, more sophisticated settlements and perhaps those which were centres of estates, lay in the valleys while the poorer and perhaps dependent farmsteads and hamlets remained largely unchanged on the upland marginal land.

It is also important to note how often, considering the difficulties of discovery and excavation, evidence of later Roman occupation occurs under modern villages and hamlets. More and more material is coming to light showing that the sites of many if not most of these were occupied in the later Roman period at least. The tessellated pavement of a Roman building has been found under the nave of Wimborne Minster church; both Wareham and Sherborne show evidence of substantial occupation; remains of a Roman building were found under the church at Tarrant Crawford in the Tarrant valley; Roman occupation has been found at Beaminster on the higher reaches of the river Brit; extensive Roman occupation has been found in and around the hamlet of West Holme on the south bank of the river Frome, within the south Dorset heathland.

Unbelievably, it was not until 1962 that it was noticed that the church of Whitchurch Canonicorum, on the south side of the vale of Marshwood in the far west of the county, has large quantities of Roman bricks incorporated in its fabric indicating the existence of a substantial Roman building near by. Even near the centre of the east Dorset heathland at Mannington, which is a scattered group of farms in a small valley, fourth-century occupation material has been discovered. These examples can be multiplied by the score and they must mean that many of the most favourable settlement sites, in the geographical sense, were not cleared from the waste by people in historic times but were already occupied by the middle of the Roman period at least and in some cases perhaps much earlier. So by the third century A.D. the picture of settlement in Dorset is one of considerable occupation of the river valleys and low-lying areas, except where precluded by very heavy soils, together with perhaps a rather sparser occupation of the higher upland parts.

In the fourth century a contraction of settlement on some of the higher lands appears to have taken place. There is evidence that some of the more primitive farmsteads in the remote and less attractive parts were being abandoned. At Woodcutts, already mentioned, the whole farmstead was abandoned about A.D. 370, a site on the downs above Bere Regis was deserted in the mid-fourth century and at a number of other places the picture is the same. Of course other settlements do remain inhabited until the end of the fourth century at least and perhaps even longer, though judging by the finds they decline in material prosperity. There is some evidence, as will be noted in the next chapter, that some of these upland settlements were never abandoned. Nevertheless, it is important to note that this contraction of settlement does take place and especially that it begins before the formal end of the Roman period. Otherwise it is easy to assume that the

37

abandonment of these sites had some connection with the Saxon settlers. This is not so.

This withdrawal of settlement from the uplands and its concentration in the lower parts of the county was in the main quite unrelated to the coming of the Saxons. It would have taken place had they never arrived and in fact was probably related to technical and geographical factors rather than racial ones. The technical advances are perhaps the most significant though least understood. There seems little doubt that by the fourth century at the latest new agricultural techniques and especially the use of a heavy plough were enabling new land in the valleys and the lower parts to be taken into cultivation and settled. There is of course no evidence of contemporary fields in these areas for they have been obliterated by later cultivation, but the existence in the archaeological record, not only of parts of these ploughs, but of other iron tools such as axes and saws, shows that clearance of relatively heavy land was technically possible and probably undertaken. Certainly the rash of occupation sites dating from the third and fourth centuries A.D. in the lowlands suggests that this work was going on. Thus there was less necessity for the expanding population to move up to the high chalk and limestone hills and work the thin soils there. They could occupy the newly cleared parts of the more fertile lowlands and valleys. At the same time there are indications that other factors were influencing the settlements on the marginal uplands. For with the clearance of the lower lying areas and improved drainage there was, especially in the chalk areas, a lowering of the water-table. Perhaps by the middle of the Roman period and certainly by the end it had become difficult, even by digging deep wells, to obtain a regular supply of water on the higher chalk downs. Therefore by the fourth century there were not only physical reasons for people to leave the uplands but technical reasons why they could settle more intensively in the valleys.

The remains of fields cultivated by the Romano-British peoples often support this idea, for where they survive they are by no means confined to the higher areas, but extend down the valley sides in many places until cut short by later cultivation. In some cases at least they may well have been worked by people living in the valleys and not on the hill-tops.

If this is true we are starting to see something resembling a 'medieval' landscape pattern with settlement and meadow in the valley bottoms, arable land on the valley sides and parts of the higher ground, and with pasture beyond. We have no idea how such settlements organised their lands for we do not know and perhaps will never know what kind of tenurial and economic units existed at this time. The parallel with the medieval pattern might mean that something similar to the typical medieval Dorset estate already existed at this time. The parallel may not be exact and it is not suggested that all the medieval manors of Dorset are necessarily exactly the same economic units as those of the late Roman period. Yet there are indications that many features of the medieval landscape were coming into being in this period. This is of special importance when we move on to the early medieval period for as we shall see there is singularly little evidence of substantial Saxon settlement in Dorset. Therefore it seems much more likely that it was the Romano-British people of Dorset, whom we know occupied the county in relatively large numbers, who laid the foundations of the medieval landscape rather than a limited number of Saxon settlers.

SELECT BIBLIOGRAPHY

Royal Commission on Historical Monuments (England). *Dorset*, Vols. I–V (1952–70 and forthcoming), hereafter R.C.H.M. *Dorset*.

Dorset

Proceedings of the Dorset Natural History and Archaeological Society (in progress), hereafter *Dorset Procs.,* for many important excavation reports, notes and studies.

Calkin, J. B. 'The Bournemouth Area in the Middle and Late Bronze Age', *Arch. Journal,* Vol. 119 (1962).

Field, N. H. *et al.* 'New Neolithic Sites in Dorset', etc., *Procs. Prehistoric Society,* Vol. 30 (1964).

Hawkes, C. F. C. 'Britons, Romans and Saxons in Cranborne Chase', *Arch. Journal,* Vol. 104 (1947).

2. The English settlement

The Saxon conquest. Saxon estates and villages.
The problem of continuity. Village shapes and fields. The early
Church and the landscape

The Saxon conquest

AS HAS ALREADY been suggested there is evidence that the Saxon[1] conquest and settlement of Dorset was relatively late in time and carried out by few people, at a stage when the supposedly medieval landscape of the county was already in process of formation. We must now look in detail at these features. In east and south-east England the evidence for the Saxon settlement comes from three main sources; archaeology, i.e. the burial sites of the earliest settlers; place-names, i.e. the names of the earliest settlements; and the early part of the *Anglo-Saxon Chronicle* which gives us a documentary version of certain aspects of the Saxon conquest. In Dorset none of these sources is very helpful. The numbers of early Saxon burials are few, there are virtually no obvious early Saxon place-names and the *Anglo-Saxon Chronicle* hardly mentions Dorset. On the other hand there is some unusual archaeological and documentary evidence which can help us.

The available evidence, slight though it is, and this is significant in itself, can be used to support a coherent picture of the Saxon conquest of the county. Burial sites and place-names in the adjacent counties of Hampshire and Wiltshire, and references to places and events in those counties in the *Anglo-Saxon Chronicle*, indicate the main lines of

[1] The term Saxon is used here without any racial significance as to whether these people were Saxons or Jutes.

Saxon advance into south-central England. It appears that the main landing places of the Saxons were in the Southampton–Portsmouth region probably towards the end of the fifth century but perhaps slightly earlier. From here they spread out north and north-east across Hampshire and Wiltshire until they met other Saxon peoples advancing from the upper Thames valley. So by the middle of the sixth century at the latest the Saxons occupied most of the chalk lands of Wessex outside Dorset. Subsequently, their main line of advance seems to have been west and then south and by the late sixth century they had conquered Gloucestershire and were moving into Somerset. But during all this time Dorset was not conquered. How can this be explained?

Certainly in the early stages of the advance from the Southampton area the vast expanse of the New Forest and the east Dorset heathland, west of the river Avon, may have protected Dorset. But with Wiltshire under Saxon domination there was no reason why the Saxons could not have swept south-west from the Salisbury region across the Dorset downs. They did not, and the reason for this almost certainly lies in the existence of Bokerley Dyke, a huge linear defensive earthwork which stretches from the densely wooded part of Cranborne Chase in the extreme north of the county along the county boundary until it reaches the edge of the heathland of north-east Dorset, a distance of some six miles. It thus completely blocks the main route from the north into Dorset. It was built originally before the end of the Roman period around A.D. 370 in order to block the Dorchester–Salisbury Roman road and the chalk downlands on either side of it. This work has been plausibly dated to A.D. 367, a year of severe Saxon raids all over England. It was subsequently dismantled and the Roman road reopened. The Dyke then remained out of use for a considerable, but unknown, length of time before it was refurbished and the Roman road blocked again, this time for ever.

Archaeology fails us with any dating, but it seems very likely that the Dyke was used as the main line of defence for Dorset against the Saxons of the north during the late fifth and early sixth centuries. Behind it the Romano-British peoples of Dorset continued to exist for nearly 200 years after the formal end of the Roman period. This means that the apparent process of the making of a 'medieval' pattern of settlement which we have seen in progress before the end of the true Roman period could have continued largely unaffected by outside interference.

It may be wondered why there was no attempt by the Saxons to land on the coast of Dorset. The answer may lie in the inhospitable nature of that coast. With the exception of Poole Harbour, which has a relatively unattractive hinterland, there are very few places where a massive landing could have taken place, and these could have been defended without great difficulty. Indeed there is some evidence of Saxon landings on this coast. A single cremation burial not closely dated is known from the east of Bournemouth at the mouth of the river Stour and more important the burial of a warrior dating from perhaps A.D. 450–550 has been found on Hardown Hill, not far from the sea, near Charmouth in the south-west of the county.[2] But otherwise there is nothing. The large Romano-British population of Dorset seems to have managed to keep the Saxons at bay for many generations.

However, the people of Dorset could not hold back the Saxons for ever. Sometime, perhaps late in the second half of the sixth century, the line of Bokerley Dyke was finally broken and the Saxons advanced into the north of the county. Six Saxon burials, unfortunately difficult to date, but probably late sixth century, have been found inserted into prehistoric barrows south of Bokerley Dyke on Oakley Down near Pentridge, at Knowlton and at Long Crichel.

[2] Evison, 'The Anglo-Saxon Finds from Hardown Hill', *Dorset Procs.,* Vol. 90 (1969).

Dorset

But the victory was not a complete one. The Romano-British people did not abandon the fight but merely retired fifteen miles south-westward to another defensive line. This is the linear earthwork known as Combs Ditch which runs for some three miles across the central Dorset downs on the ridge between the Stour and the North Winterborne valleys. While its tactical situation above the river Stour is excellent its overall strategic position is not as good as that of Bokerley Dyke. Combs Ditch too has been excavated and its final phase dated to a time in the post-Roman period, and probably quite late in that period. There can be little doubt that it represents another line of defence after Bokerley Dyke had been broken by the Saxons.

How long Combs Ditch lasted as a defence is not known, but it was probably manned for a short time only. Soon after A.D. 650 the Saxons appear to have broken though the ditch and reached the Dorchester area, where one of their warriors was buried at Maiden Castle. Having reached the coast the Saxons had thus split the Romano-British people of the county into two groups, one in west Dorset and the other in south-east Dorset. The former group was then apparently quickly overrun by Saxons moving west from Dorchester and also south from Somerset, and by 658 the Saxons had defeated the British at the battle of Penn, plausibly suggested by Professor W. G. Hoskins as Pinhoe near Exeter. The details of the final conquest of west Dorset are as yet unknown to us, but there is some slim evidence to indicate the final end of the encircled Romano-Britons of south-east Dorset. It would seem that they were driven right back into the heathland there, where they were finally overcome. The curious, and as yet undated, Battery Banks immediately west of Wareham which run for a distance of four miles along the ridge-top between the Frome and the Piddle rivers may well belong to this final stand of the Romano-Britons here (Fig. 3).

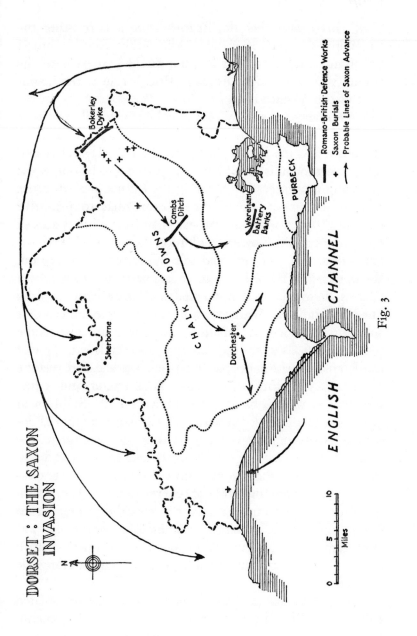

DORSET : THE SAXON INVASION

Fig. 3

Romano-British Defence Works
Saxon Burials
Probable Lines of Saxon Advance

Bokerley Dyke

Sherborne

DOWNS

Combs Ditch

CHALK

Dorchester

Wareham
Battery Banks

PURBECK

ENGLISH CHANNEL

0   5   10
Miles

All this means that the Britons were still resisting the Saxon invasion well after the middle of the seventh century, but in any case there can be little doubt that parts of the county were still under Romano-British rule at the beginning of the seventh century.

Two other points of interest may be made with regard to south-east Dorset at this time. First, it was centred on Wareham and the Isle of Purbeck. The rich clay valley and high limestone hills of the latter are proving to be one of the most populous areas of Dorset in the Roman period. More Roman settlements of all types from villas to primitive farmsteads are known in Purbeck than in any other area of comparable size in Dorset. In addition there were also important stone, shale, pottery and salt industries in the region. What area was more likely to resist the final attack by the Saxons than this well populated and reasonably wealthy one? Secondly, at Wareham not only is there evidence of substantial Roman occupation, but there are also some remarkable finds which indicate that, even in defeat, some of the Romano-British people lived on in peace and relative prosperity with their conquerors, as at Exeter, much further to the west. For at the church of Lady St Mary at Wareham is preserved a series of Christian memorial inscriptions or tombstones dating from the seventh to the ninth centuries, two of which are British in form and epigraphy. Further, there is now little doubt that the remarkable Saxon church, probably of seventh-century date, which stood on the site until 1840 was a rebuilding of an earlier Celtic church or monastery. Therefore, not only was Wareham an important and long-lived Romano-British centre but in it Romano-British people lived on alongside their conquerors.

There is evidence that Wareham was not an isolated example of this integration between Saxons and Romano-Britons. As Sir Frank Stenton pointed out many years ago, one of the laws of King Ina (688–726), probably enacted in 694, showed that "men and women of British descent had been incorporated into early Wessex society."[3]

To summarise the importance of the conquest period of Dorset, though we are accustomed to seeing the end of the Roman period as being early in the fifth century, it is clear that in fact it was well into the second half of the seventh century before the Saxon domination of the county was complete. Therefore, for perhaps over 250 years after the end of Roman rule most of Dorset remained a Romano-British rather than a Saxon sphere of influence, and in some parts rather longer.

There is still, however, the question of the racial and social impact of the Saxon conquest to be considered. The political effect is obvious, but from the point of view of the history of the landscape it is important to ask just how many Saxons settled in Dorset and how, if at all, they affected its landscape? Was there an almost complete replacement of Romano-British people by the Saxons? Did the Saxons kill or drive out the majority of the Romano-British people they defeated, leaving only a few to be integrated? Superficially, on the evidence of place-names it would appear that they did. There are relatively few true Celtic place-names in the county and the majority of these are topographical names of hills and rivers, not of settlements. Those that are Celtic habitative names are scattered fairly widely from Chideock in the south-west, Dorchester, Little Mayne, Friarmayne and Broadmayne in the south, Creech, Lytchett Minster and Lychett Matravers in the south-east and Chettle and Pentridge in the north-east. No significant pattern can be deduced from such a distribution.

It is necessary, however, to make a note of one feature of many Dorset place-names which might alter this rather

[3] Stenton, *Anglo-Saxon England* (1947), p. 311; *see also* Stevenson (ed.), *Asser's Life of King Alfred* (1904), pp. 248–9.

indeterminate picture. Most of the river names of Dorset, e.g. Iwerne, Stour, Frome, Cerne, Tarrant, are of Celtic origin. Many of these rivers have settlements along them whose early names were the river name itself. Thus there were eight settlements all called Tarrant along the river Tarrant and seven called Frome along the river of that name. All these settlements might be said to have Celtic names and if this is accepted the distribution and numbers of Celtic place-names are radically altered. They then cover the whole of the county with the exception of the extreme north and north-west and the eastern heathlands, and in numbers constitute some twenty per cent of all the places named in Domesday Book. This idea may not be readily acceptable but it is important to note how often even true Celtic place-names tend to be associated with rivers or water. Dorchester itself is one.

Even so, this still leaves some eighty per cent of the place-names of Dorset solidly Saxon. How far does this indicate a large Saxon population? Until recently it has always been assumed that such evidence did indicate this. However, certain scholars have pointed out that this is not necessarily so. Mr Loyn has said that "evidence is mounting for the transmission of British place-names during a bilingual period and there are definite signs of bilingualism on the part of the Britons, who made their names known to the Saxons."[4] Indeed it is of some interest to see how easily at a later date Dorset place-names could and did change. There are a large number of place-names with post-Norman Conquest personal names prefixed to -*ton* whose earlier names are unknown but whose existence as settlements long before 1066 cannot be doubted. Bryanston near Blandford, Godlingston in Swanage and Chaston near Buckland Newton are examples of this. If such changes could occur

[4] Loyn, *Anglo-Saxon England and the Norman Conquest* (1962), p. 12, *see also* John, *Orbis Britanniae* (1966), pp. 126–7.

following the Norman Conquest, which we know involved only a new ruling class that had little effect on the landscape, it seems not unlikely that the same kind of change could have occurred at the time of the Saxon conquest, and perhaps for the same reason. For there is no doubt that the Saxons soon had political and tenurial control of the county they had conquered. One of the earliest extant Saxon charters for which a reliable text has survived is dated 704 and records a grant of land near Fontmell Magna south of Shaftesbury by Coinred, father of King Ina. It shows without doubt that the tenurial control of the land had passed to the Saxon aristocracy, but says nothing about the Romano-British peasantry who presumably continued to work that land.

Similarly, the Saxon rulers, once Christianised, introduced their own ecclesiastical organisation, for the diocese of Sherborne was created around 705 and the first bishop, Aldhelm, came to south Dorset at least once to dedicate a church, probably at or near Corfe Castle. But again, except at Wareham, our picture of the churches of the Romano-British people is dark.

The overall picture of the Saxon conquest of Dorset is then of a relatively small warrior aristocracy imposing its political, tenurial and ecclesiastical organisation on an existing Romano-British peasantry. If this is a correct view there seems no reason to suppose that these Saxon warriors made any major changes in terms of the overall settled landscape whose outlines had been determined many years before. With this in mind we can move on to examine the Dorset landscape in the true Saxon period, A.D. 700–1066.

Saxon estates and villages

When we come to what is usually called the Saxon period it is possible for the first time, to obtain a more detailed picture of settlement in the county. Not only have we an exceptionally large number of detailed Saxon land charters to help us, but there is at the end of this period that incomparable document, Domesday Book. From these sources, from modern and old maps and, most important of all, from the existing landscape, we can not only see how well filled and organised the landscape was by the eleventh century, but also that much of the pattern was already well established by that date.

For example, we know from Domesday Book that a village called Didlington, now Didlington Farm in Chalbury parish, was in existence by 1086 and already one of a line of settlements lying along the river Allen near the western edge of the east Dorset heathland. Today the boundaries of the parish of Chalbury can be seen both on modern maps and on the ground, enclosing a roughly triangular shaped piece of land, extending from the river Allen which forms its western boundary across rising chalkland and until it reaches the heath at the eastern apex. Didlington lay along the edge of the river, where the earthwork remains of the former village can still be seen. It is clear from a charter of A.D. 946, whereby King Edred granted to a thegn called Wulfric five hides of land at *Dydelingtune,* that the parish as we see it today was then in existence. If the boundaries carefully described in the charter as being the land of Didlington were fixed by the mid-tenth century, there is reason to suppose that the boundaries of the adjacent parishes were also fixed by this time. And there is proof of this in at least one case, for Horton, immediately north of Chalbury, also has a charter dated 1033 when King Cnut granted seven hides to a thegn called Bovi. The boundaries given in this charter again agree exactly with those of the modern parish. There can be no doubt therefore that the modern ecclesiastical parishes in this part of the county were delimited long before the eleventh century.

Other charters show that many other parts of Dorset

were similarly organised. Charters such as that for Tarrant
Hinton show that the typical pattern of the present chalkland parishes of relatively long narrow strips of land running
across or on one side of the valleys was fixed by the tenth
century at least. Similarly, charters for Marnhull and
Hinton St Mary show that parishes in the Blackmoor Vale
were in existence by the same period or earlier and charters
for Thornford and Halstock in the north-west of the county,
and Corfe Castle in the Isle of Purbeck indicate that parishes
in these areas were already defined. In fact from the evidence
of the thirty or so Saxon charters that survive for the county,
it may be asserted with confidence that the great majority
of parishes in Dorset were in existence long before the
Norman Conquest and only where modern changes have
taken place is the picture any different from that in the tenth
century.

However, though most parishes, or what we now call
parishes, were fixed by the tenth century at least, this is only
part of the picture. There are often more complex internal
divisions within the present parishes which had also been
fixed by this time. In most cases there are no charters to
help us see them, though the evidence remains on the
ground and on maps for those who know what to look for.

We can start with a fairly simple example of this kind of
internal boundary, where indeed a charter proves the point.
This is at Piddletrenthide, north of Dorchester (Fig. 4).
The present parish, excluding the area of Plush to the north-
east which is a modern addition, is a large rectangular
block of land lying across the valley of the river Piddle,
entirely upon chalk. The village of Piddletrenthide is strung
out along the bottom of the valley on both sides of the river.
In fact the parish and village are very typical of all the
chalklands.

There can be no doubt at all that the boundaries of this
parish existed as we see them today by the tenth century at

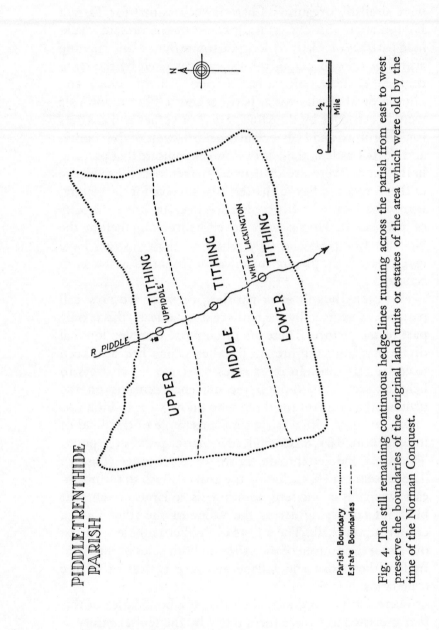

Fig. 4. The still remaining continuous hedge-lines running across the parish from east to west preserve the boundaries of the original land units or estates of the area which were old by the time of the Norman Conquest.

the latest. The eastern boundary was certainly fixed by the early tenth century for it is described in a charter of 1019 for the adjacent parish of Cheselbourne and part of the northern boundary is described in a charter of 891 giving the bounds of Plush. As we shall see, we also can be sure that the rest of the northern boundary of the parish and part of the western boundary were also in existence by 966. By 1086, Domesday Book records the existence of the village of Piddletrenthide assessed for thirty hides, from which of course it gets the latter part of its name. However, there is also a charter for Piddletrenthide itself. It is dated 966 and by it King Edgar confirmed to Shaftesbury Abbey the possession of ten hides of land at a place called *Uppedelen* (perhaps meaning Up or Upper Piddle). The charter boundaries are difficult to work out in detail, but there can be no doubt that they describe a block of land lying across the river Piddle and comprising the northern third of the present parish. While the north, east and west boundaries of this land coincide with the present parish boundary, the southern boundary is marked today by an almost continuous hedge-line which runs right across the parish from east to west. This means that in 966, and perhaps for a long time before, the northern third of the parish was separate from the rest. But we can go further. The southern two-thirds of the parish is also divided into two by another continuous hedge-line running from east to west. Thus the modern parish appears to be made up of three separate and similarly sized land units. These units still existed as major agricultural boundaries as late as 1817 for when the common-fields of the parish were finally enclosed by Act of Parliament there was not one common-field system but three. Each of these quite separate common-field systems lay within the three suggested land units. These land blocks are called on the enclosure map Upper, Middle and Lower Tithing respectively. With this in mind, if we now look more carefully at the long sprawling village of Piddletrenthide, it becomes clear that there are three settlements, each still physically separate. In the north is a group of houses round the church and the manor house within the area called Upper Tithing which must be the *Uppedelen* or Uppiddle of the charter. Further south is another group of houses lying within Middle Tithing, and south again in Lower Tithing is a third group, now called White Lackington.

So from the evidence of charters, maps and the ground it is clear that long before 1066, what we now call the parish of Piddletrenthide was already laid out into three compact land units each associated with a small settlement. By 1086 the original three units (perhaps assessed at ten hides each?) had become one tenurially and have remained so up to this day, but the more important economic division was to remain intact for much longer.

Once we grasp the evidence described in detail above, of long continuous hedge-lines still surviving in the modern landscape, defining blocks of land each associated with settlements already in existence by 1086, we can reconstruct large areas of the tenth- and eleventh-century landscape of the chalklands of Dorset. The late C. D. Drew showed this was possible many years ago in an article on parishes in the Iwerne valley.[5] In fact most of the larger parishes of the chalk areas can be shown to have once been divided up into separate land units.

Two further examples, one fairly simple and one rather complex, must suffice for these chalklands. The first may be seen in the parish of Gussage St Michael, which is a wedge-shaped area of land of some two and a half thousand acres lying mainly on the north-east side of the valley of the Gussage brook, south-west of Cranborne (Fig. 5). The present village lies in the valley bottom near the south-east corner of the parish. Further upstream is a scatter of farms

[5] Drew, 'The Manors of the Iwerne Valley', *Dorset Procs.,* Vol. 69 (1948).

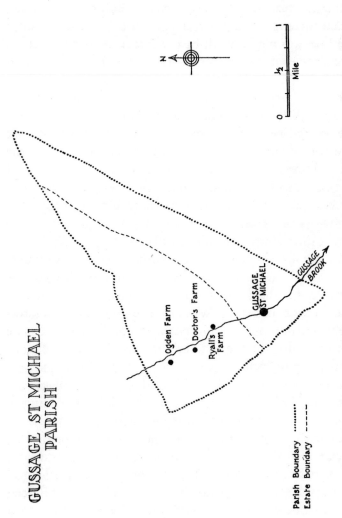

GUSSAGE ST MICHAEL
PARISH

Ogden Farm

Doctor's Farm

Ryall's
Farm

GUSSAGE
ST MICHAEL

GUSSAGE BROOK

N

0   ½   1
Mile

Parish Boundary ....
Estate Boundary ‒ ‒ ‒ ‒

Fig. 5. The long continuous hedge-line across the parish is the original boundary between two separate estates which have kept their identity since early Saxon times at the latest.

whose names of Ryall's, Doctor's and Ogden Farm are apparently of no great antiquity for they do not occur in documents before the eighteenth century. However, between these farms and the village is a continuous modern hedge-line running north-east right across the parish. Further, the enclosure map of 1814 shows that the common-fields of the parish then enclosed were confined to the part of the parish south-east of the continuous hedge-line and associated with the village. The common-fields north-west of the hedge-line, if they ever existed, had disappeared long before the nineteenth century. All this indicates that the parish originally consisted of two separate settlements and their associated land units. Though both were known from 1086 tenurially as Gussage St Michael, economically they were always separate.

A far more complex example of the same pattern may be seen in the upper part of the North Winterborne valley, west and south-west of Blandford Forum (Fig. 6). Here the modern and indeed medieval parish pattern is relatively simple. Three parishes, Winterborne Stickland, Winterborne Clenston and Winterborne Whitchurch, each lie across the valley of the Winterborne brook. At first sight there is little to indicate a complex pattern. Stickland and Whitchurch are both relatively large compact villages by Dorset standards. Clenston, while no longer having a village, has an exceptionally fine manor house and a small, late church dedicated to St Nicholas some distance away, each with a small group of cottages near them. In addition, all the parishes have other farms and houses scattered along the stream. Here we have no charters to help us, nor indeed are enclosure maps any assistance. There appears at a glance to be little of interest in the area, and what there is seems difficult to interpret.

However, from modern maps, backed by a fine eighteenth-century estate map of most of the area, and more particularly

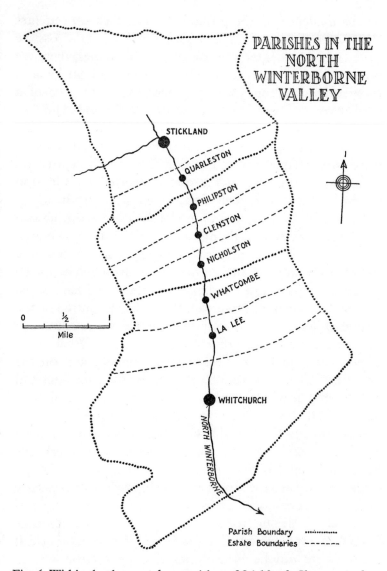

Fig. 6. Within the three modern parishes of Stickland, Clenston and Whitchurch, long continuous hedge-lines and the remains of former settlements indicate the older division of the area into small estates and hamlets which were later grouped together into convenient ecclesiastical units, probably in the twelfth century.

by the evidence on the ground, we can pick up our first clues. As well as the long continuous hedge-lines across the valley which mark the present parish boundaries, there are others of the same type. In the south part of Stickland a long hedge-line cuts off and defines the north side of a narrow strip of land in the centre of which stands Quarleston Farm. To the south in Winterborne Clenston there are two internal continuous hedge-lines dividing the parish into three almost equal parts. The northern part is centred on Clenstone Farm, the middle one is centred on Clenston manor house, an extremely fine sixteenth-century building, while the southern land unit is centred on the church of St Nicholas, which, though built only in 1849, is on the site of a medieval structure. South again in Winterborne Whitchurch are two more continuous hedge-lines which divide the parish into one large and two small land units. The largest, occupying over half the parish, is centred on the village of Whitchurch. North of it lie the two smaller units centred on the hamlets of Higher and Lower Whatcombe respectively. So from the evidence of maps, and on the ground, there are indications of not just three parishes and villages but a whole series of land units associated with separate settlements of a now familiar pattern.

If we turn to the available documentary evidence we can go further and identify these settlements. Winterborne Stickland cannot be identified in Domesday Book, though it certainly existed then for there is a slightly earlier reference to it in a French document of 1068–84. Quarleston again is not identifiable in 1086, but appears as Winterborne Quarel in 1232 named after the Quarel family who held it then. There can be little doubt that Quarleston was in existence in 1086 and must be one of the unidentified Winterbornes of Domesday Book. Similarly we can see that the northern land unit in Winterborne Clenston is that called Winterborne Philipston from 1244, the centre

unit is that known as Winterborne Clenston from 1232, and
the southernmost as Winterborne Nicholston from 1283.
Moving south again into Whitchurch it is clear that the
northern land unit was known as Winterborne Whatcombe
from 1316 onwards. The centre land unit can in fact be
identified in Domesday Book as the Winterborne held by
Milton Abbey, and was known as Winterborne La Lee
from 1244. The name La Lee was subsequently transferred
to a relatively modern farm and the original settlement took
the present name of Lower Whatcombe. The large land unit
in the south must have always belonged to Winterborne
Whitchurch.

All the evidence therefore points to the fact that what
are now three parishes were once carefully divided between
eight separate settlements, each associated with its own
distinct block of land. One further piece of evidence is the
fact that also on the ground there are, or were before
recent destruction obliterated the greater part of them, the
earthwork remains of partially deserted or shrunken medieval settlements at Stickland, Quarleston, Philipston, Clenston, Nicholston, Whatcombe, and La Lee giving added
weight to the picture revealed from hedge-lines and documents.

The same pattern of settlement and associated land units
is repeated almost everywhere else on the chalk. In the
Tarrant valley north-east of Blandford, the eight existing
parishes were once divided into twelve land units each with
its own settlement. The parish of Charminster north-west
of Dorchester can be shown to have had ten land units and
settlements within its boundaries and Sydling St Nicholas
further north-west to have had six.

So far we have concentrated entirely on the pattern of
settlements and land units on the chalklands, but this
pattern was not confined to the chalk alone. In fact it can
be seen perhaps most clearly in the Isle of Purbeck, where

it is on limestone and clay as well as on chalk. Here not only are the land units small, but almost the whole of the pre-Norman landscape is recoverable. Again hedge-lines, earthwork remains of shrunken settlement, place-names, modern and early maps, Saxon charters, Domesday Book and other documents all help in elucidating the pattern.

One detailed example in Purbeck must be sufficient, and probably the best is that of the southern part of Tyneham parish in the extreme west of the Isle. In this area there are four small settlements, each recorded by the thirteenth century under their present names. Three of them lie in the bottom of the deep, wooded, clay valley between the high chalk and limestone hills on either side. In the centre is the small village of Tyneham while to the north-west lies Baltington Farm and to the north-east North Egliston Farm. Further south beyond the limestone ridge, on a low plateau overlooking the sea, is yet another farm called South Egliston. Now Domesday Book lists not one but four places called Tyneham, but does not record Baltington or the two Eglistons. It seems certain, therefore, that three of these Tynehams are in fact the three present farms, and thus all four settlements were in existence by the late eleventh century. In addition, each of these settlements lies near the centre of a block of land clearly defined today by modern hedge-lines which run across the area from ridge-top to ridge-top. There is also evidence that both Baltington and North Egliston were once hamlets and not just farms, for around both are earthworks which include the remains of house sites and gardens. Further, in each of the four land units there are extensive and extremely well preserved remains of medieval cultivation strips which carefully respect the continuous hedge-lines and nowhere cross them. So once again there is proof of complete and careful division of part of what is now a parish into separate land units and their settlements, apparently at a very early date.

This arrangement is repeated in the rest of the Isle of Purbeck (Fig. 7). Steeple parish east of Tyneham can be seen to have been divided between the settlements of Steeple, Lutton, Hurpston and Blackmanston; Kimmeridge parish between Kimmeridge, Smedmore and Little Kimmeridge; Church Knowle parish between Church Knowle, Whiteway, Barnston, Bucknowle, East Bradle, West Bradle, East Orchard and West Orchard, etc. In total the eight parishes or parts of parishes which lie south of the north Purbeck Ridge contain nearly fifty settlements and their land units, all in existence before the Norman Conquest.

Turning to the heathland areas, we again find a well organised and developed pattern of settlement and land units, though because of the nature of the country and the resulting small settlements a somewhat different pattern emerges. In east and north-east Dorset for example the heathland is of a gently rolling nature uninterrupted by any large rivers. A multitude of small streams, in wide open valleys flow generally east and south-east and along their courses is a scatter of farms. The villages that do exist here are relatively modern creations. Few of the scattered farmsteads are of any architectural interest or antiquity and none have remains around them to indicate that they are former villages or hamlets. Neither are there any very obvious continuous straight hedge-lines which, as we have seen, are so characteristic of the chalk and elsewhere. Nor can the remains of medieval common-fields help us here. There are none, and indeed it is unlikely that they ever existed here.

There is, however, evidence that some of these farms are of great antiquity. Once again we can begin with a fairly simple example which has a Saxon charter to help us. The charter, dated 956, is a grant by King Edwig to Alfred, one of his nobles, of an area of land called *Uddingc*. It is of some interest to note that the land is actually described in the

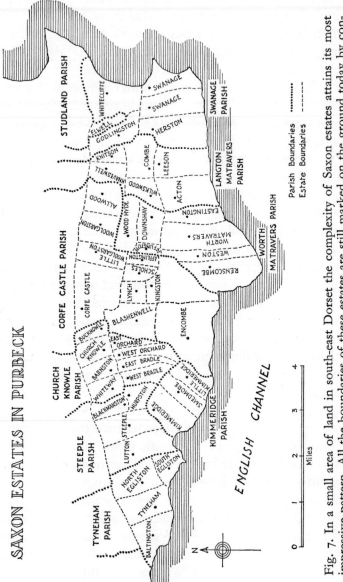

Fig. 7. In a small area of land in south-east Dorset the complexity of Saxon estates attains its most impressive pattern. All the boundaries of these estates are still marked on the ground today by continuous hedge-lines.

charter as a *hiwisc* or one family holding. We are here dealing with one single farm. There is no doubt that *Uddingc* is the modern Uddens, now a mid-eighteenth-century house with its surrounding park in the parish of Holt, two and a half miles north-east of Wimborne Minster. Until the late nineteenth century when the parish boundaries of the region were altered, this house and park were a detached part of the parish of Chalbury which lies three miles to the north-west.

The bounds of Uddens or *Uddingc* attached to the charter, though difficult to work out, for some of the landmarks given are not very clear, do in fact describe the exact bounds of the detached part of Chalbury parish. They are thus giving the bounds of a small estate or farm in the middle of the heathland in existence by the tenth century.

If we accept that one such estate could have existed at this time in the heathland we can soon find more. A further two and a half miles north is another small piece of land, clearly defined by somewhat irregular boundaries, in the centre of which is a scattered group of farmsteads collectively called Mannington. From the tithe map of Gussage All Saints parish, which lies just over four miles away on the chalk downlands, we learn that this area was once a detached part of that parish. Mannington is listed in Domesday Book as a normal small manor of two hides held by a sub-tenant of the Count of Mortain, and with three villeins and two bordars recorded as living there. This quite usual entry apparently disguises the fact that Mannington was not a village nor even a hamlet, but just a scattered group of farms lying along both sides of the Mannington brook. For there is no documentary evidence at all for a hamlet or village. In the few documents referring to it that survive, such as thirteenth-century charters and inquisitions, it is clear that it was a group of separate holdings leased from Tarrant Crawford Nunnery. There is no indication of any former common-field system either in documents or on the ground, nor are there any earthwork remains indicating a shrunken or deserted village.

Therefore by 1086 at the latest, a well defined area of land on this part of the heathland was being worked by a group of people living in isolated farms and tilling the small irregular fields we can still see there today. This pattern seems to be repeated again and again in this part of the county. There is another small block of land four and a half miles east of Wimborne on the county boundary now known as St Leonard's Common. This was the land of a single farm called Rushton, in medieval documents, which was until the late nineteenth century a detached part of Cranborne parish. Long ago C. D. Drew noted that this Rushton was almost certainly listed in Domesday Book as the formerly unidentified *Langeford,* and was worked by two villein farmers in 1086.[6]

In south and south-east Dorset the same pattern of settlements and land units exists, but here it is more akin to that of the chalklands. This is due largely to the fact that, unlike east Dorset, the heathland in this part of the county is cut by two relatively large rivers, the Piddle and the Frome, both of which have extensive river terraces along their courses. Here there is a tendency for fairly large villages to occur along the sides of the rivers, associated with generally rectangular parishes extending from the river banks across the heathland beyond.

However, these parishes are not as simple as they first appear. The parish of Moreton, seven miles east of Dorchester provides a good example (Fig. 8). The parish of just over 2,000 acres lies on the south side of the river Frome and is entirely on heathland except near the river where there are river terraces. The present village of Moreton lies near

[6] Drew, 'The House of St Leonard's, Rushton', *Dorset Procs.,* Vol. 64., (1943).

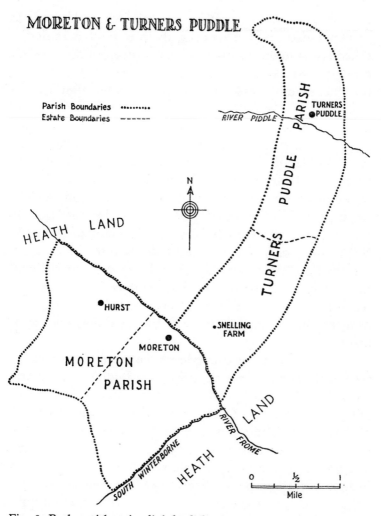

Fig. 8. Both parishes, in slightly different ways, show the internal divisions of old estates or land units centred on small settlements in the heart of the south Dorset heathland.

the north-east of the parish close to the river, and is recorded
in Domesday Book. However, there is another settlement
called Hurst in the parish, a mile north-west of Moreton and
also close to the river. The name Hurst is not recorded in
documents until 1318 but not only is its position identical
with that of Moreton but it is clear that it was once associated with a land unit quite separate from that of Moreton.
For there is still a continuous hedge-line running almost
the whole length of the present parish dividing it into two
parts, with Hurst at the north-east end of one and Moreton
at the north-east end of the other. In fact it can safely be
assumed that both settlements existed by the eleventh
century, for there is not one entry for Moreton in Domesday
Book but two. The larger, a manor of three hides with a
recorded population of nine, must be Moreton itself, while
the other, a manor of one hide and eight acres with a
recorded population of seven, must be Hurst. So again we
have evidence suggesting early land division and settlements.

A slightly different example of the same pattern can be
seen in the adjacent parish of Turners Puddle to the north-
west (Fig. 8). The parish of nearly 2000 acres covers a
fairly narrow strip of land running south-west to north-
east across the heathland. From the river Frome on the
south, it extends northward across the heathland to a ridge
and then into the valley of the river Piddle crossing it to
include a further piece of heathland on the north bank.
Within the parish are two settlements of some antiquity.
North of the Piddle, close to its bank is Turners Puddle
itself, now comprising only a church and a farm, and in the
extreme south of the parish on the banks of the river
Frome is Snelling Farm. Turners Puddle was certainly in
existence by 1086 for it must be one of the many Piddles
recorded in Domesday Book. It is then reasonable to suggest that the land on either side of the river Piddle was the

land unit of Turners Puddle, and by the same token, the land between the Piddle–Frome ridge and the river Frome ought to be the land of Snelling Farm. Unfortunately Snelling Farm is not recorded as such until the fifteenth century but both names Snell and Snelling are well attested Old English personal names and thus the settlement may be older than its first documentary appearance. In fact it may well be one of the unidentified 'Fromes' of Domesday Book.

When we turn to one of the major clay areas of the county, the vale of Blackmoor, the same fact emerges. By the eleventh century it is clear that though the landscape here is still relatively empty of settlement, there is no doubt at all that it was already divided up into major land units. To deal with the settlements first, it is important to examine their general siting, for they do not always appear to obey the normal 'geographical' rules that one would expect in an area of exceptionally heavy clay land. While the positions of many of the modern villages seem at first to have been determined by the underlying geological conditions, this is not always so. For example, the villages in the centre of the vale of Blackmoor, from Todber in the north, through Marnhull, Hinton St Mary, Sturminster Newton, Fifehead Neville to Haselbury Bryan are all on the low Corallian Limestone escarpment, with extensive clay lands on both sides. But in these clay areas there appear to have been other settlements in existence just as early. To the south-east of the limestone ridge are East and West Orchard and Manston, while to the north-west are Lydlinch and Holwell. And again in this area there is no doubt that the present parishes were already in existence at a very early date too. There are Saxon charters for the parishes of East Orchard, West Orchard, Margaret Marsh, Marnhull, Hinton St Mary and Sturminster Newton, all dated to the tenth century or earlier and all indicating that the present boundaries were already formed by then.

67

Here too, where there was to be much subsequent settlement and land clearance, there is evidence that even by the eleventh century some parishes were already subdivided into separate land units each with its own major settlement. Thus the large parish of Stalbridge, north-west of Sturminster Newton, already comprised two separate parts by 1086 for both Stalbridge itself and Stalbridge Weston, a smaller settlement to the south-west, are recorded in Domesday Book (Fig. 9). Documents, including a Saxon charter, and the remains of the common-fields of the two settlements indicate that the boundary between the two land units is a small south-flowing stream dividing the parish into two parts. Likewise the present parish of Pulham can be seen to have been made up of two settlements, East and West Pulham, each with its own land unit (Fig. 10). And in the north of the county there is no doubt that the present parish of Kington Magna originally had two land units. The larger, covering most of the parish, belonged to Kington itself, but a small area in the south-west of the parish, which is a low clay ridge almost entirely surrounded by the water of the river Cale and the Bow brook, was by 1086 the land of two small settlements now called Higher and Lower Nyland (lit. Island).

Finally we turn to the varied landscape in the west of the county. Here too there is evidence that by the eleventh century at the latest, settlements and their land units were already fixed. In the clay Marshwood Vale as in the Blackmoor Vale and in parts of the heathlands of Dorset, there is evidence that geographical conditions led to late settlement of the area, which was not fully completed until the later medieval period. However, it was clearly under way by the eleventh century. The details of this form of settlement will be considered in the next chapter, but it must be noted here that it took place within the already fixed boundaries of what were to become parishes. Outside the heavy

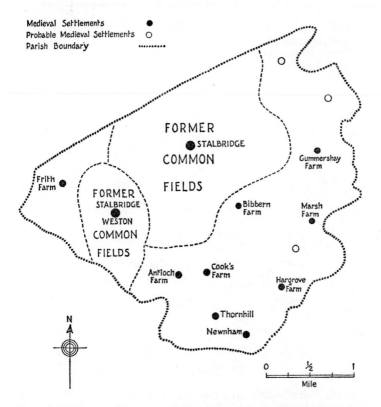

STALBRIDGE PARISH

Medieval Settlements ●
Probable Medieval Settlements ○
Parish Boundary ⋯⋯⋯

FORMER

● STALBRIDGE

COMMON

FIELDS

Gummershay
Farm

Frith
Farm

FORMER
STALBRIDGE
WESTON
COMMON
FIELDS

● Bibbern
Farm

Marsh
Farm

Anfloch
Farm

Cook's
Farm

Hargrove
Farm

N

● Thornhill

Newnham ●

0   ½   1
Mile

Fig. 9. In the wooded, clay vale of Blackmoor the two original
settlements of Stalbridge and Stalbridge Weston lie in the centres of
their former common-fields. Beyond in the once forested area are a
whole series of isolated farmsteads, most of which are first recorded
in documents of the thirteenth and fourteenth centuries.

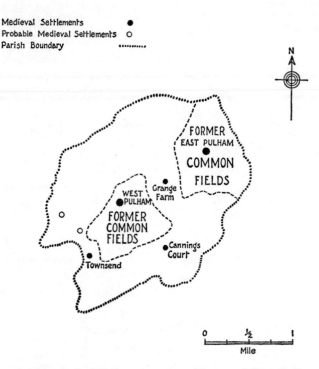

Medieval Settlements   ●
Probable Medieval Settlements   ○
Parish Boundary   ·········

FORMER
EAST PULHAM
COMMON
FIELDS
Grange
Farm
WEST
PULHAM
FORMER
COMMON
FIELDS
Cannings
Court
Townsend

0   ½   1
Mile

Fig. 10. The two original settlements of East and West Pulham are surrounded by a number of isolated farmsteads all of which came into existence during the later medieval period and were set up in the former forested areas of the parish.

clay areas the more usual pattern of early settlements and land units is clearer. Two of the Saxon charters that survive for this part of the county, both for part of Corscombe parish, confirm that even in the area of the parish on limestone and clays there is a continuous hedge-line separating the land of Corscombe itself from the land of the settlement of Catsley and a similar one separating the latter from that of the land of a place now called Benville, thus producing three early land units.[7]

So at some length we have moved round the county and examined the pattern of settlements and their associated lands which appear to have been in existence by the eleventh century at the latest. We have seen that in some cases such units are identical with the modern parishes, but more often are not. Up to now we have called these areas rather vaguely 'land units'. But what in fact are they? They must represent something more important and older than mere ecclesiastical or tenurial groupings. They must be basic farming units or estates within which are carefully husbanded the necessary requirements for subsistence agriculture with, as far as is geographically possible, areas of meadow, arable and pasture or waste. As such, they are likely to be the oldest and most necessary of all land units.

One other point worth noting here is the 'continuous hedge-lines' which we have seen mark the division between the land units. These, though of great antiquity, are usually most disappointing to look at, and belie their age. In most places they are quite ordinary hedges set on small banks and not the huge dykes which seem to have bounded many of the Saxon estates in Devon and Cornwall.[8] However, their early origin as boundaries is certain and the new

[7] Drew, 'Earnley, a Lost Place Name Recovered', *Dorset Procs.,* Vol. 71 (1950).
[8] Hoskins, *The Making of the English Landscape* (1955), pp. 55-7.

71

techniques of botanical hedgerow dating might produce valuable results here.

The problem of continuity

Having suggested that these land units were in existence by the eleventh century and earlier in some cases, we are faced with the question of when this overall pattern of settlements and land units or estates came into being? To recall what has been said in Chapter 1 and the first section of this chapter, there are a number of important points to be noted. There is the undoubted existence of lowland settlement even in the late prehistoric period. Then there is the evidence for lowland-based estates having developed before the end of the fourth century. There is the archaeological evidence of Romano-British occupation under many of the existing villages and hamlets. Then we must take into consideration a long period of possible development of the landscape that could have occurred between the end of the fourth century, when the archaeological record appears to finish, and the end of the sixth century, or in some places the middle of the seventh century, before the county was occupied by the incoming Saxons. Finally we have to note the evidence which suggests that the Saxon conquest itself was carried out by relatively few people who imposed political control on the still remaining mass of Romano-British peasantry.

We are left facing the fact that if the whole pattern of settlement and land units that we have seen existed in Dorset by perhaps the mid-ninth century is of Saxon origin, then this was achieved by a relatively small Saxon population in less than 200 years. This seems inherently improbable. We are forced to the inescapable conclusion that the basic arrangement of settlements and their estates in Dorset is likely to be Romano-British or Celtic rather than Saxon in

Plate 7 Sherborne Abbey, perhaps the finest building in the county. From the eighth century and possibly earlier men have laboured here building and rebuilding this church. Today it stands, not only as a magnificent monument to their piety and craftsmanship, but as the latest stage in the long history of the impact of the Christian Church on the landscape.

Plate 8 Knowlton church, Woodlands. The isolated twelfth-century church, now a ruin, stands centrally in a huge prehistoric religious enclosure (a 'henge'). As the soil marks in the adjacent fields show, it was once surrounded by other enclosures and burial mounds. The medieval village of Knowlton, now utterly depopulated, lay some distance from the church on the near side of the river.

Plate 9 Winterborne Tomson church. A rare survival of the small, unaisled, early medieval churches that were probably common before the great fourteenth- and fifteenth-century rebuilding.

Plate 10 Strip-lynchets, Worth Matravers. Here the common-fields of the village were extended up the hillsides at the very limits of the parish. The strip ploughing on the rising ground produced these terraces.

Plate 11 Field-remains in Compton Valence. The larger banks are the boundaries of roughly rectangular prehistoric and Roman fields. The slighter ridges within these fields are the remains of temporary medieval ploughing, probably of thirteenth-century date.

origin. This is not to say of course that we have in Dorset an *actual* Roman landscape. The settlement and estate-pattern in the county was constantly developing from prehistoric times and by the end of the formal Roman period it was beginning to take on the appearance that we have described in detail above. Further changes and developments must have gone on through the post-Roman period and were probably unaffected by the coming of the Saxons under whose purely political rule the pattern was further refined and fixed. Therefore, when the light of the Late Saxon charters and Domesday Book finally illuminates the scene we have what is normally accepted as a fully developed Saxon landscape.

Even so, there are places where it seems that there may be a direct link with the Roman period. At Hinton St Mary, north of Sturminster Newton in the vale of Blackmoor, we can be sure that the present boundary of the parish was already fixed by 944 when it was described in detail in a charter. And in the centre of the parish, on the edge of the village is the remarkable villa, discovered in 1963, which had a Christian *motif* worked into one of its mosaic pavements, dating from the mid-fourth century. Perhaps more interesting is the parish of Halstock in the far north-west of the county. Here also the parish boundaries are recorded in a charter of 847, and again a Roman villa has been discovered there.[9] But in addition the name Halstock means 'Holy Place', an indication perhaps of early religious associations. These examples can be multiplied a number of times from all over the county, and while individually they may not stand up to close historical scrutiny, collectively and with the additional evidence discussed already, they add up to an impressive picture.

[9] The problem of continuity of boundaries between Romano-British Villa-estates and those of Old English estates as set out in land-charters is still exceedingly difficult of solution, but microscopic work on local topography will one day yield results.

There remains one more interesting facet of the Dorset landscape of this period which as yet we have not looked at, but which fits into the general Celtic background of its history. We have seen in Chapter 1 how, during the Roman period, the upland areas of the county were intensively occupied, perhaps for the first time, and also how many of these were later abandoned. There are, however, existing settlements that look suspiciously as if they are some of these upland Roman settlements which have survived until the present day. The classic example of this type of settlement, noted by O. G. S. Crawford and W. G. Hoskins, is the village of Ashmore which lies high on the north Dorset chalk downs.[10] It is in fact situated near the end of a south-projecting spur at over 700 feet above sea-level and its only means of existence until relatively recently was the large embanked pond which lies in the centre of the village. Its name is purely Saxon and no Roman finds have, as yet, been discovered there. But there can be little doubt that the village is one of many upland Romano-British settlements. It survived perhaps by reason of its ever-filled pond which most other Romano-British settlements lacked (Plate 6). Perhaps the most telling evidence of its early origins is to be seen by comparing its position to those of the known Romano-British settlements of the surrounding areas. It is of great significance that most of them lie in very similar positions on spur-tops.

However, though Ashmore is always cited as a living upland village on the site of a Romano-British one with probably a continuous existence for at least 1600 years, it is by no means the only one. Especially in the general region round Ashmore are further examples. The hamlet of Wood-yates, strictly East Woodyates, in the extreme north of the county far from any stream, actually lies on top of a Roman posting-station and other finds of Roman occupation have

[10] Hoskins, *The Making of the English Landscape* (1955), pp. 42–4.

been made at the near-by Woodyates Manor and its hamlet of West Woodyates. In addition it is possible that the village of Handley near by to the south-west has similar Roman origins, for though the modern settlement lies in the two arms of a now dry valley it is significant that the church and what is apparently the original nucleus lie on the crest of a spur between the arms in a similar position to Ashmore.

Elsewhere in the chalk areas of the county are other possible upland Romano-British villages still in existence. A fine example is the two adjacent farms of East and West Hemsworth in Witchampton parish north-west of Wimborne Minster. Both are listed in the Domesday Book. And not only are there the remains of a remarkably well preserved deserted medieval village at East Hemsworth, but just north of West Hemsworth a particularly fine Roman villa was found in the nineteenth century. Outside the chalk areas of the county are other villages whose siting is worth noting in this context. For example North and South Poorton, north-east of Bridport, are two adjacent villages set in a most 'un-Saxon' position on the top of a small plateau above deep south-west-draining valleys. All these settlements, and a number of others, may well be the surviving relics of the upland extension of Romano-British settlement.

Village shapes and fields

Unlike many places in England, Dorset does not have any well marked village forms, except of the simplest kind. 'Green' villages and those with complex street plans are rare, and the single street type of settlement sometimes with a 'back-lane' is almost ubiquitous. In part this is almost certainly the result of the small size of the great majority of Dorset villages, but in addition many settlements lie within narrow valleys where there is often little room for more than a single street.

Many of the villages in the chalk areas, and indeed in the limestone regions too, reveal this basic street form. Tarrant Keynston and Turnworth are good examples. Where the valleys are wider there is a tendency for a street to develop on both sides of a stream, though such a feature is not always recognised because one of the streets has often been partially abandoned, as at Piddletrenthide. Where there are relatively wide valleys, or where two or more valleys meet, village plans tend to be more complex, but there is little more than obvious significance in the resulting pattern of streets. At Beaminster, a large village by Dorset standards, its position at the head of the valley where four streams meet in a wide basin results in a street plan almost directly related to the natural routes along these streams.

Of the villages which take up more complicated forms, the interest lies in being able to remove the modern and even late medieval development and reveal their earlier lay-out. The apparently formless pattern of a village such as Haselbury Bryan in the vale of Blackmoor, which consists of an incoherent sprawl of dwellings and roads scattered over an area of nearly three miles, becomes meaningful if the area is examined in this way. The later medieval expansion of settlement in this wooded area is reasonably well documented, and for the post-medieval period can be worked out from the date of many existing buildings. It soon becomes clear that there were once three small single-street settlements about a mile apart, boasting the unlikely names of Kingston, Wonston and Droop.

Likewise at Morden on the northern edge of the south Dorset heathland, there is a similar pattern of scattered dwellings and narrow lanes. A careful study of the area reveals a much simpler and apparently older lay-out consisting of at least four hamlets lying along streets, which probably may be equated with four of the five separate entries under that place-name in Domesday Book.

Finally we must mention the field system of this early period, if only in a negative sense. A few years ago, in a book of this nature, this chapter would have included an account of the appearance in the Saxon period of the well-known open-field or common-field system with its pattern of long narrow unfenced strips divided between two or more large fields and worked in common.

We can no longer be sure, however, that such a system was introduced, fully developed, by the Saxons and it may be that it was a feature which developed gradually over the centuries after the coming of the Saxons. Indeed, if this be true, such an idea would fit in well with the suggestion put forward above of the Celtic nature and origins of the Dorset settlement pattern. For if the land units and settlements are basically of a Celtic rather than Saxon origin, there is some reason to suppose that the land itself was worked in a basically Celtic way. Unfortunately we have no idea of what kinds of fields existed in the Roman period in the low-lying areas of the county for it is precisely these areas which have been continuously cultivated throughout the historic period, obliterating all that came before them. There is evidence on the upland areas that the normal square or near-square fields of the prehistoric and early Roman period were being superseded by rather elongated fields in later Roman times, though these are still a long way from a medieval common-field arrangement. There seems no reason, however, to suppose that the 'normal' common-field system as generally understood arrived with the Saxon conquerers of Dorset and it may be that it was developed gradually in the centuries following their arrival.

In addition it may be noted that in many places there is no evidence that common-fields ever existed, even where we know there was very early settlement. For example, there are clear indications that there were never any common-field systems in the whole of the east Dorset heathlands though, as pointed out above, there were certainly settlements before the eleventh century. The occupants of the heathland farms and hamlets seem always to have cultivated enclosed fields, much as they do today, and indeed it is likely that some of these actual fields originated before the eleventh century.

The early Church and the landscape

Though on the whole we have so far not emphasised the importance of the ecclesiastical units or parishes in the landscape and have concentrated on their earlier economic basis, the early Church nevertheless played its part in the making of the Dorset landscape. Apart from two or three Roman sites which have produced archaeological evidence apparently of Christianity, such as the villas at Maiden Newton and Hinton St Mary, the visible effect of the Christian Church does not appear until the establishment of Saxon rule in the county. Then the effect is marked and still visible.

The most important aspect was the establishment of large 'minster' churches which initially at least seem to have been under the control of semi-collegiate groups of priests who were jointly responsible for the spiritual welfare of large areas of land around these churches. It was not until much later that these large territories were gradually superseded by the parish church as we know it, with its single priest responsible for one settlement or for a small group of adjacent settlements.

It is possible in Dorset to go some way towards establishing the sites and also, in part, the original large 'parishes' of some of these early minsters. Minsters undoubtedly existed in some of those villages which today still retain the word *minster* in their name. These are Beaminster, Charminster, Iwerne Minster, Sturminster Marshall, Sturminster Newton, Yetminster and Wimborne Minster. In addition, however, it is possible by detailed documentary work, sometimes aided by architectural evidence, to establish the identity of other former minster churches whose adjacent settlements have not retained or even acquired the name *minster*. Such places are Sherborne (Plate 7), Wareham Lady St Mary, perhaps Whitchurch Canonicorum, and Canford Magna. At the latter for example, not only does one version of a late twelfth-century charter state that the church was formerly held by a clerk and two other people, which suggests a small ecclesiastical community there, but the greater part of the nave and crossing of a minster church of about 1050 survives in the chancel of the present church.

More interesting, perhaps, in terms of the total landscape is the evidence for the large territories served by these minster churches. Even on a map one is struck by the large sizes of the present-day parishes of some of them. Beaminster and Sturminster Newton are good examples of this. Also Charminster parish, whose territory, as we have already noted, contains ten medieval settlements and their land units. But documentary evidence makes it possible to take this further. It can be established that Sturminster Marshall, a relatively small parish little larger than those around it, was once much larger (Fig. 11). For even in the nineteenth century the present parishes of Corfe Mullen and Lytchett Minster and the former parish of Hamworthy, now part of Poole, were all parochial chapelries of Sturminster. Indeed the name Lytchett Minster indicates that it was the Lytchett that belonged to the minster in contrast to the other Lytchett (Matravers) which once belonged to the family of that name. The shape of the boundaries of Lytchett Matravers suggests, however, that this parish too was once part of the territory of the minster.

In this part of the county one can virtually reconstruct all the land of the early minster churches. North-east of

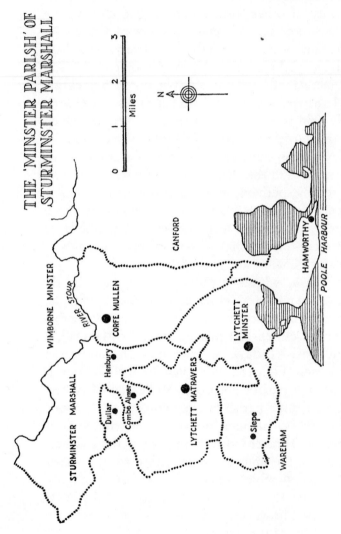

THE 'MINSTER PARISH' OF STURMINSTER MARSHALL

Fig. 11 The area shown in the diagram is almost certainly that of the original 'minster parish' of Sturminster Marshall. It is surrounded on all sides by other 'minster parishes' and up until the mid-nineteenth century Corfe Mullen, Lytchett Minster and Hamworthy were parochial chapelries of Sturminster. The present parish boundaries are probably even older than the 'minster parish' for their curious arrangement suggests that places such as Dullar, Combe Almer, Henbury and Slepe are centres of old estates.

Sturminster lies Wimborne Minster which until as late as 1894 had a parish of nearly 12,000 acres covering not only the present town but the modern parishes of Colehill, Pamphill and Holt and including a host of small medieval settlements, many of which were in existence by the late eleventh century. South again, up until the nineteenth century, the parish of Canford Magna covered a vast area of land which today includes most of the borough of Poole and part of the county borough of Bournemouth. If the use of nineteenth-century evidence may be thought somewhat late to show a connection with an eleventh-century minster, we can turn to a document of 1256 where Canford church is described as having "the chapel of Pola [Poole] and the other chapels belonging to the said church."

Within these minster church territories were sometimes standing crosses, often on or near the sites of the later parish churches or parochial chapels, at which services were conducted in the early days. These were once probably extremely common in the county and it is of some interest that in the ninth-century life of St Willibald, written by a nun of Wessex origin and therefore perhaps familiar with Dorset or the adjacent areas, it is noted that on the estates of many lords there was no church but only a cross.[11] The remains of a number of these pre-conquest crosses still exist, though they are not always easily found or recognised. Part of a tenth-century cross is now used as a font in Melbury Bubb church while the fine early eleventh-century cross-head at Cattistock is hidden in a recess in the chancel of the church there.

As time went on parish churches gradually replaced these crosses. These were built usually by local lords to serve the needs of communities on their own estates, and this is why so many churches lie adjacent to the premier manor house of the village. The result today is often a most delightful

[11] Quoted by Stenton, *Anglo-Saxon England* (1947), p. 150.

grouping of church and manor house which is an especially attractive feature of the county. It may be seen well at Mapperton near Beaminster where the tiny, unaisled, medieval church is actually connected to the beautiful seventeenth-century manor house.

In other places, however, the siting of the church may be due to older and more mysterious reasons. The best known example is at Knowlton, in the east of the county, where the church lies, not in the village, now deserted, but 300 yards away within the encircling bank and ditch of a prehistoric 'henge' or ritual monument (Plate 8). Likewise at Moreton, in the heathland of the south-east, the church stands on a large mound which might well be a prehistoric burial place. Such positions must reflect a continuous use of sites of religious significance over thousands of years even if the churches themselves were built in only the eleventh or twelfth centuries.

Because of the scattered nature and small size of the settlements many of the new churches came to serve more than one settlement with the result that their parishes emerged by the grouping of the older economic land units to produce the present, often complex, pattern.

The process of establishing parish churches was slow, and was certainly not completed even by the late eleventh century. It is impossible to assess how many churches existed by this time. Apart from the minsters, there is architectural evidence of pre-conquest churches at only Winterborne Steepleton, Studland and perhaps at Bere Regis. Domesday Book records a number of churches in existence by 1086 but this is almost certainly not a complete list. As well as those which were minsters, Domesday mentions churches at Wareham, Bridport, Burton Bradstock, Chaldon Herring, Dorchester, Fleet, Gillingham, Puddletown and Winfrith Newburgh. Further, priests are recorded at four other places though whether churches existed there is unknown.

During the twelfth century more churches seem to have been built, and many probably rebuilt, for many in Dorset have architectural evidence of this period. Particularly fine is the tower of Lyme Regis church, but perhaps a better example of what a typical twelfth-century church must have looked like is that at Winterborne Tomson. Here there is a virtually unaltered, tiny, single-cell building with a characteristic apsidal east end (Plate 9).

One other feature of the pre-conquest landscape was the monastic establishments. There were large ones such as Abbotsbury, Cerne, Shaftesbury and Milton, and smaller houses such as Cranborne and Horton. At none of these, however, are there any structural remains of this period, nor did they seem to have any great effect on the landscape in the estates that they owned. Not until later centuries did their effect on the landscape become marked.

SELECT BIBLIOGRAPHY

Fägersten, A. *The Place Names of Dorset* (1933).
Finberg, H. P. R. *The Early Charters of Wessex* (1964).
Grundy, G. B. 'Dorset Charters', *Dorset Procs.*, Vol. 55 (1933)—Vol. 61 (1939).
Hawkes, C. F. C. 'Britons, Romans and Saxons in Cranborne Chase', *Arch. Journal,* Vol. 104 (1947).
Hoskins, W. G. *The Westward Expansion of Wessex* (1960).
R.C.H.M. *Dorset.*

3. The countryside fills up

Villages, farms and fields. The development of the medieval Church. The homes of lords and peasants

IN A GENERAL sense we have covered the story of the Dorset landscape up to the late eleventh century, a convenient point to stop because of the picture that Domesday Book affords us. We must be careful, however, not to regard 1086 as an important break. In terms of the landscape the date means nothing. The Norman conquerors of our county had little direct or immediate effect on the landscape which continued to evolve in its own way. We must be careful too of Domesday Book itself for its interpretation is fraught with difficulties. Because it was compiled on a tenurial basis there are severe limitations on what it can tell us about the contemporary countryside. It says little, and then very indirectly, about the basic land units which, as we have seen, existed long before 1086. By no means all of the settlements in existence at that time are recorded by name, nor is much light shed on the ancient ecclesiastical pattern of large minster parishes in the process of being replaced by the complex of small church parishes.

Nevertheless, Domesday Book *is* an invaluable document which can tell us much if used with caution. Its greatest value lies not in giving a picture of the landscape in 1086, but, with the help of other documents and features still visible on the ground, in giving us a view of the landscape before and after 1086. The picture that it gives us in 1086 is usually not detailed enough for our purposes but it does imply important general patterns into which we can fit our more detailed knowledge. In the chalklands, Domesday Book reveals the lines of valley-bottom settlements that had long been in existence, and from the limited amount of arable recorded suggests that much of the area was not intensively cropped. The use of the higher parts of the downs for sheep is well brought out, for not only are extensive tracts of pasture listed, but large flocks of sheep sometimes running into many hundreds per manor are recorded in the Exeter version of Domesday Book. In the heathland areas, Domesday Book indicates clearly that there was little land under cultivation but that large areas of pasture existed. However, it almost certainly understates the actual amount of settlement in these areas.

Similarly, in the clay and limestone parts of north-west Dorset and particularly in the varied landscape of the west, while Domesday Book rightly shows that extensive forests were to be found, the intensity of settlement is again probably seriously understated.

It is this inadequate picture of settlement that is Domesday Book's greatest weakness. Accepted at its face value it provides us with a view of the late eleventh century which is virtually that described in the previous chapter. This being so, for the period after 1086, we are presented with an impression, based on a mass of documentary evidence, of a fairly rapid increase in population and attendant expansion of settlement into the so-called marginal areas until then largely uninhabited. This impression is to some extent true, but not entirely so. The documents of the twelfth and thirteenth centuries can and do mislead us. They record numerous settlements and hundreds of acres of arable land as appearing for the first time in these centuries. Yet it has to be remembered that most of these records first came into being at this time. Thus the earliest appearance of a named farm in a thirteenth-century document may be misleading.

The chances are that many such farms are much older than their first appearance in a document.

Occasionally even Domesday Book indicates this by chance. It appears from documents that many of the isolated heathland farms in the south-east and east of the county came into existence in the twelfth and thirteenth centuries. But by a tenurial accident Domesday Book records the existence of a single farm, Hethfelton (Heath Farm), in a most exposed and inhospitable position high on the windswept heath in East Stoke parish. Similarly, there is evidence both on the ground and in documents for a great extension of arable land in the twelfth and thirteenth centuries. Again by chance, the entry for Swyre in Domesday Book contains a most unusual phrase which implies an extension of arable land into former pasture. Neither of these examples is likely to be an isolated instance and they urge caution in the use of both Domesday Book and other later documents to interpret the landscape.

Our problem, and it is largely insoluble, is therefore to decide how much of what appears to be new in the Dorset landscape of the twelfth and thirteenth centuries is really of that date and how much is actually far older. It is probably true to say that the pattern of settlement and land units discussed in the previous chapter was established by the ninth century and perhaps even earlier. Subsequently, within that basic framework, there was a continuous process of infilling of new settlements which went on until the mid-fourteenth century in most places. It is this filling up of the rural landscape which we will now look at in detail.

Villages, farms and fields

Once again no overall picture of the growth of settlement and of farmlands is possible. We must still examine what happens in the various parts of the county. Within the chalkland areas virtually no new settlements were developed within the existing pattern, largely because settlement was restricted by its need for water to the valleys which were already occupied by lines of villages and hamlets. Any increase in population could only take the form of an expansion of the existing sites. It is clear from evidence on the ground that this is what actually happened in many cases, for what were once sharply separated hamlets later became almost continuous lines of settlement along the valleys. The reality is, however, more complex than this and there are indications that even by the thirteenth century some places were already declining in population. The details will be considered in the next chapter; here it is enough merely to note the problem. The overall impression is one of gradually increasing population, of which we may obtain some indication, however approximate, by comparing the population of places recorded in Domesday Book with the taxpayers listed in the mid-fourteenth century Subsidy Rolls. These sources provided recorded, not absolute, figures of population and since they were gathered on differing bases, they are not directly comparable. The Subsidy Rolls are also certainly under-estimates, since we know there was a great deal of tax evasion in this period as well as legitimate exemption. In some Leicestershire villages we know that two-thirds to three-quarters of the households do not appear in the 1327 tax lists. These instances may be exceptional, but often we can be sure that half the population escaped notice in these records.[1] But these figures are all we have, and they do indicate what was taking place. The hamlet of Monkton Up Wimborne, now in Wimborne St Giles parish, has a population of nine listed in 1086, but in 1332, seventeen taxpayers or heads of families are recorded. Similarly at the hamlet of Ash in Stourpaine parish, the population in 1086 is seven while by 1332 fifteen taxpayers are listed.

[1] W. G. Hoskins, *Provincial England* (1963) pp. 182-3.

In agricultural terms there is evidence of an increase of arable land in the chalk areas. By the thirteenth century common-field agriculture existed over most of the chalk and there are clear indications of its gradual expansion, though not by any means closely dated. One of the major features of the present landscape which probably originated at this time and represents, at least in part, the extension of arable are the so-called *strip-lynchets*. These are the long narrow terraces, often arranged in flights extending up the hillsides (Plate 10). Though they have been interpreted as vineyards, etc., they are in fact nothing more than the extension of the normal medieval common-field system on to sloping ground.

Whether these terraces are formed by plough action alone or, as seems more likely, in part by deliberate construction, they represent difficulties in terms of pure agricultural techniques. It was surely no easy task to plough such terraces or even to reach them. Thus their cultivation would have been undertaken only when flatter, more easily-worked land was already under the plough. To some extent strip-lynchets must represent land-hunger in the face of a steadily rising population. They are therefore most likely to date from the twelfth and thirteenth centuries or slightly earlier. They occur widely in the chalk areas, though they are most obvious where the natural slopes are greatest and thus the 'risers' or faces of the terraces are highest. As a result there are many good examples all along the face of the chalk scarp across central Dorset especially at Buckland Newton, Woolland, Ibberton, Sutton Waldron and Compton Abbas. But other fine examples exist elsewhere on less steep ground, for instance along the valley of the South Winterborne associated with the settlements of Winterborne Came, Monkton and Steepleton.

A further feature of the rural landscape of this period, now unhappily rare because of recent destruction, is a type

Plate 12 The heathland of south-east Dorset, immediately north of the Purbeck Ridge. The irregularly-shaped fields in the centre of the photograph
were carved out of the heath before the Norman Conquest, for the farm
within them is West Creech which was worked by one villein and one bordar
in 1086. Elsewhere the more rectangular fields and their associated small
cottages date from the late eighteenth and nineteenth centuries. The photograph also shows how the heathland encroaches on the fields if they are left
uncultivated for any length of time.

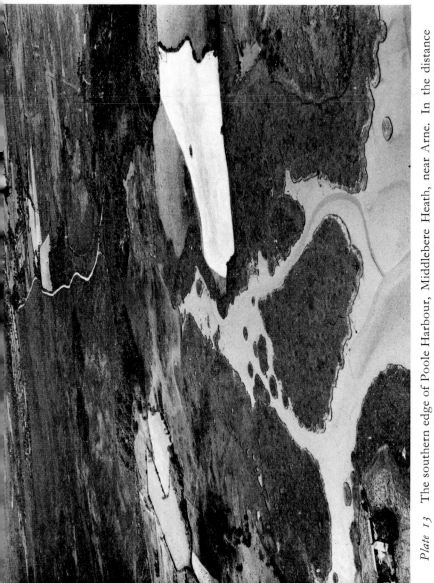

Plate 13 The southern edge of Poole Harbour, Middlebere Heath, near Arne. In the distance is the present edge of arable land which has been slowly extended into the heath for over 1000 years. The small, irregular fields along the water's edge in the foreground belong to a series of farmsteads such as Middlebere Farm in the bottom left hand corner. Both forms and

Plate 14 This photograph, of part of Pulham parish in the vale of Blackmoor, shows the irregularly-shaped fields so typical of the claylands of the county. They were formed by the gradual enclosure of the forest and waste throughout the medieval period. The farm in the top left is Grange Farm which once belonged to Bindon Abbey and is first recorded in 1237. The pattern of narrow lines in some of the fields is nineteenth-century drainage, a good indicator of the heavy nature of the clay soils here.

Plate 15 Corfe Castle and village. The remains of Dorset's greatest castle still dominate the stone-built houses of the village which grew up under its protection. The castle, originally erected by William the Conqueror and constantly rebuilt and enlarged, was finally reduced to its present state

of ridge-and-furrow which occurs on the tops of the high chalk downlands. It resembles that found elsewhere in England, though here on the downlands the ridges are only a few inches high. This is in part because of the light soils which prevented the ridges from being built up to any height, but, more important, it is due to the very temporary nature of the cultivation. It is fascinating too to see that some of this downland ridge-and-furrow often lies on top of earlier Roman and prehistoric fields which can clearly be recognised under the later ploughing. This again indicates the temporary nature of such cultivation. How such short-lived extensions of the medieval common-fields were worked is quite unknown. They are not dated at all in Dorset, though examples in Wiltshire have been ascribed to the thirteenth century. The best example of this type of field-remains existed until recently in Compton Valence parish, west of Dorchester (Plate 11). They covered forty acres of high downland called the Great Field and were quite separate from the permanent common-fields of the village in a valley to the north. Other examples still survive at Turnworth and Alton Pancras.

Though it appears that common-field agriculture was practically ubiquitous in the chalklands, this does not mean that the landscape was totally hedgeless. Not only were the valley-bottom meadows enclosed, but there is abundant evidence for enclosed pastureland on the chalk downs. Unfortunately, its precise position is rarely specified in documents, but it probably lay on the downlands beyond the common-field arable. Such "pastures several throughout the year" as they are usually described are recorded at many places in the thirteenth century. These pastures were probably connected with sheep farming which was important in the area by the eleventh century at least. Even the incomplete figures of sheep given in the Exeter version of Domesday Book show this well. They include flocks of

1600 sheep at Puddletown, just over 1000 at Cranborne and over 800 at Ashmore, and for the succeeding generations there are many documents recording flocks of sheep on the chalk downs.

Chance has on a few occasions provided us with the evidence of temporary human occupation of the high downs which was probably associated with the sheep farming. On Oakley Down in the north of Wimborne St Giles parish, modern ploughing has turned up the remains of a small two-roomed stone building with a yard apparently of the thirteenth century. It was undoubtedly a shepherd's hut.

In the heathland parts we are presented with a very different picture. We have already noted that there is evidence for groups of small farms in east Dorset, and small villages in south-east Dorset prior to the eleventh century. It is certain that the population in these heathlands grew between 1086 and 1350 for we have figures that show this. For example, at Morden on the north side of the south Dorset heathland the recorded population of thirty in Domesday Book may be compared with the forty-three taxpayers listed in the Subsidy Rolls for 1327. In fact the various documentary sources taken at their face value suggest a massive expansion of settlement and farming in the form of isolated farmsteads and their enclosed fields during the twelfth and thirteenth centuries.

The parish of Bere Regis lies on the northern edge of the heathland, half on chalk and half on heath, across the valley of the river Piddle (Fig. 12). Bere Regis, clearly the original settlement of the parish, lies alongside the river, just on the chalk, and had until the nineteenth century its common-fields lying to the north of it on the gentle slopes of the downs. But Domesday Book records two other settlements as well as Bere Regis in existence by 1086. These are Shitter-ton, a hamlet west of Bere Regis, and Dodding's Farm, south of the village, both again on chalk near the river.

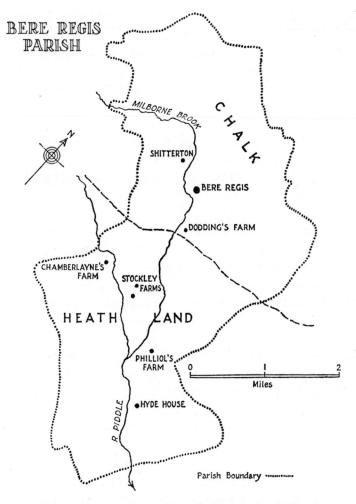

Fig. 12. The village of Bere Regis and its adjacent settlements of
Shitterton and Dodding's Farm, all recorded in Domesday Book,
lie in the chalklands of the parish. Beyond, out in the heath, is a
further scatter of isolated farmsteads whose existence is recorded
in thirteenth-century documents, but which are probably much
older.

These are secondary settlements of Bere Regis, founded before the eleventh century. But further south-east along the river and all in the heathland are a whole series of isolated farmsteads such as Chamberlayne's Farm, two Stockley Farms, Philliol's Farm and Hyde House, all of which are recorded for the first time in various twelfth- and thirteenth-century documents. Further, the making of some of the irregular enclosed fields which still surround these farmsteads is actually recorded in the mid-thirteenth-century Forest Eyres.[2] The latter list fines paid for the enclosing of fields from the waste, or 'assarting' as it was called, for this area which formed part of a royal forest at this time. In 1257 Henry de Stock (of Stockley Farm?) "made a purpresture of one acre enclosed by a hedge" and seven other people are also recorded as enclosing a total area of sixteen acres in the same year. We may take this evidence at its face value and say that all these isolated farmsteads and their fields are post-eleventh century in origin.

It is possible, however, that some at least of these farmsteads are much earlier. This is suggested by evidence from elsewhere which indicates that other isolated farms were in existence on the heathland by 1086. We have already noted the establishment of Hethfelton Farm on the heath by that date, and in other places too the same feature is discernible. Further south across the heathland is the 'village' of Povington, in Tyneham parish. It is recorded in Domesday Book as a manor of eight and a half hides with a demesne farm worked by eight slaves and with four villeins and five bordars as tenants. But Povington is not a normal nucleated village. It consists of a group of scattered farmsteads lying on the heathland at the foot of the north Purbeck ridge. These farmsteads are of interest not as

[2] Unpublished Forest Eyres (Public Record Office, E. 32/10 (1257) and E. 32/11 (1269).

buildings but from their sites and associated land. Up to the nineteenth century there was one large farm with just over 230 acres of land, four smaller farms each with between forty and seventy acres, and eight or nine smallholdings each with a cottage and from five to fifteen acres of land. Professor Hoskins has pointed out that in all probability the large farm is the demesne farm of Domesday Book and that the four smaller farms are the holdings of the four villeins recorded there.[3] It is further possible that some of the smallholdings are those of the bordars. If we accept this we are faced with the situation that most of the present farms were in existence by 1086. The fact that there are too many smallholdings does not invalidate the argument. In this area it is obvious that from an early date people were reclaiming land from the heath to cultivate and settle on.

Domesday Book is merely giving us a picture of the process in the middle of its development. It was a process that was old by 1086, and which went on throughout the rest of the medieval period and beyond. Yet these changes are virtually undocumented except in the landscape itself. Indeed the landscape shows us how the taming of the heathland was carried out. For there is no evidence that there was ever a common-field system here. Each farmstead is surrounded by more or less irregularly shaped enclosed fields, which look as if they have been cut out of the waste one by one. Here then we have evidence of the early existence of isolated farmsteads in the heathland which Bere Regis could not provide, and yet there is no reason to suppose that Povington is unique. The same pattern of farms and fields is repeated all over the heathland and Domesday Book can often help us to establish the half developed picture of 1086 (Plate 12).

In east Dorset this same process can be detected. We have already seen (pp. 63–64) that at Mannington, Uddens

[3] Hoskins and Stamp, *The Common Land of England and Wales* (1953).

and Rushton there is clear evidence that isolated farms existed there by the Norman Conquest at the latest, and probably for centuries before. But there is also definite evidence of the continuing establishment of small farms throughout the post-conquest period, as generations of farmers gradually extended the frontiers of cultivation (Plate 13).

Immediately north of Wimborne Minster there is a large area of heathland covering some twelve square miles, now represented mainly by the parish of Holt. Until modern development occurred, this tract contained only the small hamlet of Holt, eight farms and thirty-odd smallholdings surrounded by small irregularly shaped fields stretching up towards the open heathland. For this area Domesday Book records three small manors, two called Petersham of three virgates and one hide respectively, the latter with eleven bordars, and one called Thorn Hill of half a hide, with five bordars. By analogy with Povington these ought to represent three farms and perhaps sixteen smallholdings. Today there is one farm called Petersham and one called Thorn Hill and there was until the eighteenth century another Petersham Farm. On the other hand three other existing farms, Honeybrooke, Grange and Bothenwood Farms, as well as Holt hamlet, are all first recorded in the fourteenth and fifteenth centuries. Because the entries in Domesday Book appear to be single farms and must account for the Petersham and Thorn Hill Farms, the others must have come into existence between the eleventh and fifteenth centuries. They therefore represent the continuous expansion of settlement and agriculture in this part of the heathland. Once again, the existing fields show the now familiar pattern which indicates their origin, and though we have no direct evidence of the making of these fields, a little further north in the part of Edmunsham parish on the edge of the heath there is such evidence. In an Inquisition Post

Mortem of 1288 it is stated that there are thirty acres of wood there, "the wood being cut down when the land shall be assarted is worth fourpence per acre."

In spite of all the clearance of the heath, however, these farms and their fields still occupied only the more favourable places around the edges or along streams and rivers. With few exceptions the true heathland was still empty of settlement and cultivation. And yet it was not useless. It provided extensive common pasture for cattle and sheep.

Turning now to Purbeck, we find, as in the chalk areas, little evidence of new settlements in this period, for as we have already seen the area was divided up and intensively settled long before the eleventh century. So the increase in population here produced an expansion of the arable over formerly uncultivated land. Often the most difficult land was put under the plough. At Tyneham, high above the village on the steep slopes of Tyneham Cap, medieval farmers forced their ploughs across the sides of earlier prehistoric fields in order to produce strip-lynchets. Farther east at Worth Matravers the local farmers cultivated strip-lynchets at the very limits of their available land, ploughing across old landslips above the cliffs in an area fully exposed to the rigours of sea winds (Plate 10).

In north-west Dorset, where in contrast there was land to spare, this period witnessed a massive attack on the still forested claylands there. The growing population gave rise to dozens of new settlements and thousands of acres of newly cleared land. We have already noted the existence of villages all over this area, each the centre of a land unit, usually the modern parish. Most of these villages were surrounded by the thirteenth century at the latest by their common-fields, but in most cases these occupied only a small proportion of the total area of the parish or land unit. Beyond lay large areas of waste and woodland. Indeed so well wooded was the area that the Norman kings made part of it into two royal forests, Blackmoor and Gillingham, for hunting purposes. But whether in the royal forests or outside them the impact on the woodland and the waste was the same. The inhabitants of the villages gradually extended the area of land under cultivation by clearing the forest round the edges of the common-fields. While some of the newly cleared land was incorporated into the existing common-fields, the greater proportion of the new land was divided into small hedged fields. These still exist on the ground today, and their curiously irregular form with hedges often perched on massive banks indicates their mode of origin. In many cases the clearance of this land was not only carried out from the villages. People moved into the waste, built a farmstead and cleared the surrounding land. Most of these farms too exist today. Architecturally they are usually of little interest being modern 'rebuilds', but their names occur for the first time in documents of the thirteenth and fourteenth centuries. Once again it may be wrong to accept the date of their first appearance in documents as being their date of origin. It is likely that some of them at least are much older than that, but proof is lacking.

Some of the land 'assarted' or won from the forest is also of thirteenth-century date, for we have the details of it; but again it is likely that much land was cleared before this, though not documented until later. There are brief references to money paid to the crown for assarts in Dorset royal forests in the Pipe Rolls for as early as 1170-7. However, the fuller records that exist show well what was going on in the thirteenth century and indicate perhaps what had been going on for centuries before. A typical record is that in the Forest Eyre of 1269 for Gillingham Forest, when the regarders said "that Peter de la Babent occupied anew at Gillingham one acre of land of the Lord King and built upon it a house and enclosed the rest with a ditch and a hedge." All classes of society were engaged in this clearance. Only one feature distinguishes the rich from the poor and that is the amount of land cleared. One Ingelram de Berenger, who held an extensive estate in the area and who as steward of the Forest of Blackmoor was in an ideal position to clear land, was in March 1314 granted permission to "reduce to cultivation" seventy-six and a half acres of land, and in October of the same year a further 108 acres, all in Hermitage parish.[4] In 1269 the Abbot of Abbotsbury was holding nearly thirty acres of land in Hilton "which a certain predecessor of his who is dead enclosed", while in 1257 "Adam de Warner, the reeve of Marnhull, occupied in Todeber [Todber] one acre of land enclosed by a hedge."[5] At the lower end of the social scale an entry in the Court Rolls of Gillingham for 1302–3 gives a telling picture of what must have been very common. "Walter atte Wodeseyned gives to the Lady Queen twelve pence for a perch and a half encroachment opposite his gate paying for rent one penny a year."

Not everyone was happy with the encroachments in the forests. Unenclosed it was invaluable for pasture, pannage and, if it could be gained without the forest officials' knowledge, timber and deer. Sometimes, therefore, a violent objection to these encroachments occurred as at Lydlynch in 1279 when "certain malefactors and disturbers of the King's peace ... pulled down a certain ditch of Henry Baret ... with force of arms by night."[6]

Two detailed examples will show how this development of new settlements and fields affected the landscape. Stalbridge parish, as we have already seen, was before 1086 composed of two large land units, associated with the

[4] *Cal. Patent Rolls,* Vol. II (1313–17), p. 99; and *Cal. Fine Rolls,* Vol. II (1307–19), p. 216.

[5] Forest Eyres for the Forest of Blackmoor, 1257 and 1269 (Public Record Office, loc. cit.).

[6] *Somerset and Dorset Notes and Queries,* Vol. 9, No. 147.

villages of Stalbridge and Stalbridge Weston. Beyond the
cultivated land surrounding these villages lay a large area
of forest and waste. But by the mid-fourteenth century at
least eight isolated farms had been established in this
forested area, for their names are recorded for the first
time in a variety of thirteenth- and fourteenth-century
documents (Fig. 9, p. 69). These are Gummershay Farm
(1285), Thornhill (1244), Antioch Farm (1244), Newnham
(1244), Frith Farm (1244), Cook's Farm (1327), Bibbern
Farm (1327), and the lost Hyde Farm (1327). And some at
least of the irregularly shaped fields surrounding these
farms are recorded at this period too. For example in 1269
"Richard de Stapelbrigge [Stalbridge] occupied anew and
holds at Nywenham [Newnham] two acres of land . ... and
enclosed them" and "the Abbot of Shyreborn [Sherborne]
holds three acres in Stapelbrigge which a certain predecessor of his enclosed."

In the parish of Pulham further south the same pattern
is revealed (Fig. 10, p. 70 and Plate 14). The parish, mainly
on heavy clay, comprised by the eleventh century two separate land units centred on the two settlements of East and
West Pulham. By the mid-fourteenth century there is evidence of two isolated farms beyond the common-fields in the
former waste. The present Grange Farm, first recorded in
1237 as "grangiam abbatis de Byneden [Bindon]", was
set up in the waste land between the two earlier settlements,
and Townsend Farm south-west of West Pulham was in
existence by 1333. Three other farms in similar positions
may also have been in existence by then but there is no
documentary proof of this. Again, the clearance of the forest
for enclosed fields is also recorded. In 1302 there was a
lawsuit over twelve acres of land which had been enclosed
from the waste in West Pulham and in 1269 four people,
including the Abbot of Bindon, are listed as having enclosed fields from the forest.

When we study the varied landscape of west Dorset in these centuries we find much the same pattern as we have already noted both in the chalk and claylands of the county. On the limestone and sandstone hills there is evidence that the common-fields of the existing villages and hamlets were greatly extended for there are thousands of acres of strip-lynchets on the steep hillsides in positions requiring immense labour to construct and plough them. Fine examples of these may be seen in the parishes of Netherbury, Loders, and Powerstock, as well as in many other places. In addition, everywhere in the clay areas there is evidence of the extension of settlement on a large scale usually in the form of single farms. One complex example will show this. The area involved is the west end of the Marshwood Vale, a heavy wet clayland, ringed by high sandstone hills into which are cut deep narrow valleys. In this region there is only one village, that of Whitchurch Canonicorum, though there are two small hamlets, Wootton Abbas and Wootton Fitzpaine.[7] There are some indications that these three places once had common-fields around them, but elsewhere the land is characterised by small irregular fields bounded by thickly wooded hedges perched on massive banks and with narrow lanes wandering between them leading to a host of isolated farmsteads. Of these farms the great majority are all recorded for the first time in twelfth- to fourteenth century documents. The names of these farms are of some importance, for not only do many of them end in -*hay* (an enclosure), but they often incorporate a Middle English or post-conquest personal name, e.g. Bluntshay and Gummershay Farms in Whitchurch parish, Harmshay Farm in Marshwood parish and Champershay Farm in Wootton Fitzpaine. From this it might be assumed that all these farms

[7] Wootton means 'Wood-farm', indicating the nature of the country round here under natural conditions. The narrow winding lanes of this piece of country further suggest early clearance from woodland.

are of twelfth- to fourteenth-century date but this is not necessarily the case. It is not possible to correlate these farms with the villeins listed in Domesday Book as was done in Povington, but it is unlikely that the forty or more villeins together with the bordars and slaves recorded in the seven Domesday manors in the area actually all lived in the tiny village of Whitchurch and the hamlets of Wootton Abbas and Wootton Fitzpaine. Some undoubtedly occupied several of the isolated farms of which there were forty-eight in this region by the fourteenth century. Indeed, Gummershay Farm is certainly identical with the dairy farm mentioned in the Saxon charter of 1044 relating to Wootton Abbas. Again the picture is one of a gradual development of secondary settlements and their fields in difficult land, taking place over a long period of time and beginning much earlier than is generally realised. Elsewhere in west Dorset this pattern is repeated again and again. At Mapperton, south-east of Beaminster, from the original village of Mapperton two or perhaps three isolated farmsteads had come into existence by 1244 and at Burstock, west of Beaminster, at least two outlying farms had been established by 1202.

Beyond the fields and farmsteads the hills and wastes of west Dorset were already well populated with sheep at this time. Even in a small, relatively low-lying parish such as Wyke Regis, near Weymouth, the manorial Account Rolls for 1242–3 record a total of just over 500 sheep on the demesne farm and the previous year's total had been nearly 700. The same Account Roll provides evidence of an unusual form of assarting by noting that fourpence was received from "Anselm Capellanus . . . for a certain piece of land reclaimed from the sea." This must mean reclamation of marshland behind Chesil Beach.

Yet another aspect of the landscape at this time, common to all parts of Dorset, was the establishment of deer parks.[8] These were pieces of land enclosed by a park-pale, usually an earthen bank topped by a timber fence and with an internal ditch. They varied greatly in size from a few acres to nearly a thousand. Some ninety such parks are known from Dorset. None date from the pre-conquest period and it was after the Norman Conquest that they became common, for both the Norman kings and their nobles were devoted to hunting. Moreover, the parks played an important part in the domestic economy, for one of their main purposes was as a source of fresh meat especially in winter. Such parks as Blagdon in Cranborne parish, Gillingham and Rampisham were held directly by the crown. At Gillingham, for example, the park was the core of the huge royal forest there and the kings hunted deer that were released from the park. The major land-holders, the nobility and the clergy, also had similar parks; the earls of Gloucester at Alderholt and the earls of Lincoln at Canford, the Bishop of Salisbury at Sherborne just outside his castle, the Abbot of Cerne at Duntish in Buckland Newton parish and the Prior of Frampton at Earnley in Corscombe parish. Even the lesser lords also had parks such as the Cantilupe family at Stockwood near Yetminster. Traces of nearly all these still exist, often bounded by large banks. Perhaps the best preserved is that called Harbin's Park in Tarrant Gunville parish. It covers 115 acres and is completely enclosed by a massive bank with an internal ditch still clearly visible on the ground.

The development of the medieval Church

Before the eleventh century the religious houses of Dorset appear to have made little impact on the landscape, but in the next two and a half centuries some of them played an

[8] See Cantor and Wilson, 'The Medieval Deer Parks of Dorset' (Select Bibliography at end of this chapter).

increasing part in its development. The older Benedictine houses of Milton, Abbotsbury, Cerne, Sherborne and Shaftesbury all appear to have been rebuilt on a lavish scale after their refoundation, mainly in the eleventh century. There are records of twelfth- and thirteenth-century building at all of them, and though little remains today except at Milton and Sherborne, all dominated their immediate surroundings both physically and economically from the thirteenth century onwards. It is not without significance that the villages at Milton, Cerne and Abbotsbury all became large and prosperous by Dorset standards during the medieval period, and that at both Sherborne and Shaftesbury the abbeys played a large part in the growth of these towns.

All this is in sharp contrast to the three later Cistercian houses in the county. By the very nature of the order there was little attempt to influence the adjacent settlements. Bindon Abbey, even after its removal in 1172 from its original remote site at Bindon in West Lulworth parish to its final site near Wool, remained quite separate from that village and had little influence on its growth. The same is true of Forde Abbey in Thorncombe parish in the far west of the county. It too was resettled on its present site in 1141, but its position at the very edge of the parish in a remote situation had little impression on the village of Thorncombe nearly two miles away to the south-east.

At the Cistercian nunnery of Tarrant Crawford, the situation appears to be rather different, though it must be pointed out that what appears to be, for Dorset, a unique feature is not documented and therefore must remain only an inference from the present landscape (Fig. 13). The nunnery was established in 1230 by Bishop Richard Poore, a native of the village. Today the site consists of the older parish church, and a farm and its outbuildings which contain fragments of the nunnery. There are also the earth-

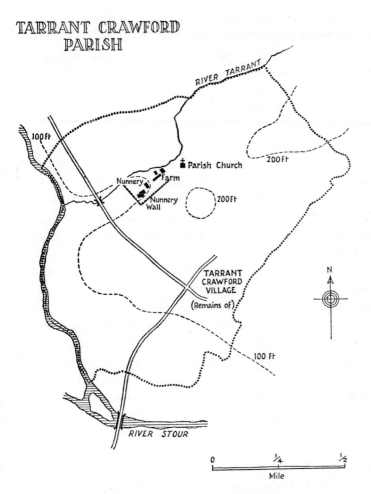

TARRANT CRAWFORD
PARISH

RIVER TARRANT

100 Ft

✝ Parish Church

200 Ft

Nunnery
Farm

Nunnery
Wall
200 Ft

TARRANT
CRAWFORD
VILLAGE

(Remains of)

N

100 Ft

RIVER STOUR

0   ¼   ½
Mile

Fig. 13. Here on a map is the only evidence for the apparent removal of the village of Tarrant Crawford from its original site near the church to its present position half a mile away to make way for the Cistercian nunnery in 1230. The village is now largely deserted, though the remains of the former house sites still exist around the cross-roads.

work remains of a precinct wall around the site. All this lies in the valley of the river Tarrant in exactly the same position as all the adjacent villages. But there is no village of Tarrant Crawford at this spot. The present village, now largely deserted, lies nearly half a mile away to the south-east, in a dry tributary valley of the river Stour, and not in the Tarrant valley at all. The village has certainly been in this position since the fifteenth century for there are the remains of a cross of that date there. It seems most likely that the original village of Tarrant Crawford lay in the Tarrant valley around its church and that it was removed to its present site to make way for the nunnery, perhaps to enable the latter to remain isolated from the outside world.

All these religious houses had extensive estates in the county, and some of the richer ones, especially Shaftes-bury, in other counties as well. Similarly, other houses outside the county such as Glastonbury Abbey and the Priory of St Swithun, Winchester, held extensive estates in Dorset. There is no evidence, however, that any of these monastic estates were exploited or worked differently from the adjacent lay estates. Much of the land was leased, though there were also grange farms worked by lay brothers. In this sense the effect of these houses on the landscape was negligible.

In addition to the religious houses, churches continued to be established in the two and a half centuries following the Norman Conquest, and certainly by the thirteenth century the parochial system was fully developed. It is difficult to see what the churches of Dorset were like at this time as the surviving remains are neither common nor impressive, thanks to the later extensive rebuilding of most of them, mainly in the fifteenth century as in Cornwall and Devon. Nevertheless certain features are clear. In general, the small size of most of the villages in the county resulted in mainly small, plain twelfth- and thirteenth-century churches, usually without aisles. Examples are widely scattered in the county from Arne and Chalbury on the heathlands in the south-east and east; Hamoon, Shillingstone, Sandford Orcas and Ryme Intrinseca in the north-west; Frome Vauchurch and Stratton on the chalk to Stoke Abbott and Chilcombe in the west. Similar churches of twelfth- and thirteenth-century date appear to have had one or two aisles added in the early fourteenth century as at Powerstock and Poynington. It was usually only in the larger villages where there was a greater population and/or perhaps more money that churches were aisled from the beginning, or were of cruciform plan. Such can be seen at Broadwindsor and Winterborne Whitchurch. Naturally there are exceptions to all this, where individual wealth or piety led to a finer church. At tiny Church Knowle in Purbeck there is a magnificent thirteenth-century cruciform church and there is a similar one at South Perrott in the west.

The homes of lords and peasants

In terms of the entire landscape the imprint of the Norman conquerors and their descendants was small. The most immediate impact of the conquest was the growth of castles from which the newly acquired land and its communications could be controlled. Though on the whole time has treated the medieval castles of Dorset unkindly, castle building was generally on a small scale. The crown certainly built three castles, and probably two others, soon after the conquest. One was at Dorchester and was intended to control the county town. No trace of this now exists. Another at Powerstock, still a fine example of a motte and bailey, was undoubtedly meant to protect west Dorset. Corfe Castle, the finest and best known castle in the county, was raised on the hill controlling the gap through the Purbeck ridge—the main route into the Isle of Purbeck—and dominated much of south-east Dorset (Plate 15). It is also probable that the crown was responsible for the tiny and still perfectly preserved motte and bailey castle at Cranborne which not only protected the royal manor there but watched over the then main road between Salisbury and south Dorset. The curious structure known as Rufus Castle at Church Ope Cove on the Isle of Portland dating from the twelfth century was also a royal castle. It seems to have performed two functions, protecting both the royal manor of Portland and the anchor passage to Weymouth Bay.

The great Norman barons of Dorset have left virtually no trace in the landscape. With one important exception none of them desired, or perhaps was allowed, a fortified residence in the county. The exception is Sherborne Old Castle, in Castleton parish outside Sherborne, built by the great Baron-Bishop Roger of Salisbury between 1107 and 1135. It shows splendidly the secular might of a great ecclesiastic, together with an emphasis on domestic comfort rather than military defence. For though the site is protected by a large moat, curtain walls and towers, together with a massive keep, these are only part of a building of decidedly residential character. The keep in fact forms only part of a central block of buildings surrounding a cloistered courtyard of non-military form and purpose. The adjacent deer park also shows that this castle was primarily a domestic residence and a symbol of prestige rather than a fortified retreat.

The civil war of the mid-twelfth century brought the county briefly into the forefront of military events. The contestants in that war were often involved in combat in Dorset and both Corfe and Powerstock castles came under attack. Just beyond bow-shot of the former there is a fine example of a ring and bailey siege-work apparently built at this time. At least two other castles, at Wareham and Shaftesbury, belong to this period. That at Wareham consisted of a large stone keep set in an earthen motte together with a bailey. Severe treatment during the civil war and its subsequent abandonment have reduced it to no more than a mound, with the bailey now marked by the curving line of a street. Of Shaftesbury Castle, a now much mutilated small motte and bailey, nothing is known beyond its mid-twelfth-century date.

After this war no truly defensive buildings appear to have been erected in Dorset for some 400 years. The few so-called castles of the thirteenth and fourteenth centuries were domestic houses or palaces surrounded, presumably for domestic prestige purposes, by shallow moats of little defensive value. King's Court Palace at Motcombe in the north of the county was a large moated hunting-lodge used by the monarch in the thirteenth century when hunting in the surrounding Gillingham Forest. Marshwood Castle in west Dorset is no more than the moated house of the de Mandeville family, barons of Marshwood between 1205 and 1264.

Moving down the social scale there is, inevitably, little evidence of the domestic buildings of lesser lords and land-holders of this period. There are no standing structures of this type before the late thirteenth century and without exception all the early farms whose history we have traced have been entirely rebuilt. The only examples are at Moigne Court, Owermoigne and Barnston Manor, Church Knowle, one containing a fine first-floor hall and the other a ground-floor hall (Plate 16). Both these buildings are of high quality and are not necessarily representative of the period. Elsewhere, changes and alterations usually prevent us from seeing what a thirteenth-century farmstead really looked like. Occasionally one can find such a place, even if the standing structures are of a later date. Such is Corscombe Court in the north-west of the county. The farm lies some way from the village in an area of heavy clay and must represent one of the later settlements in the parish established in a clearing in the forest. It is surrounded by a shallow moat, and the tiny island within it is occupied by a small yard, bounded on three sides by stone rubble farm buildings roofed with stone slates and including a fine fifteenth-century barn. On the fourth side is the farmhouse which retains some late thirteenth-century features. Here perhaps the appearance of a medieval Dorset forest farm can best be appreciated. The view north, past the stone farm buildings and across the still moat, is to small fields bounded by large banks with thickly wooded hedgerows, little changed from when they were first cleared from the forest in the thirteenth century or perhaps even earlier. To stand here is to be back in medieval Dorset.

To see and understand the typical chalkland village of medieval Dorset we must leave the existing villages and turn to the sites of those deserted in the fourteenth and fifteenth centuries. The best of these, though sadly unknown, is that of Bardolfston, near Puddletown, in the valley of the river Piddle. There, on either side of a broad hollow-way, which was the main street of the village, are at least eleven house-sites. These consist of rectangular structures defined by grass-covered flint walls up to two feet high, twelve feet to fourteen feet wide and up to thirty-five feet long. Most of them have two opposed entrances in the centre of their long sides and some have traces of an internal cross wall. These are medieval peasants' long-houses of one or two rooms, the larger perhaps originally for cattle. They stand on the street side of small 'yards' bounded by low banks, within which are small platforms no doubt the sites of outbuildings. Beyond these yards, the existence of ridge-and-furrow indicates the position of the former common-fields extending up the valley side. Nowhere in Dorset is there a better place to see exactly what a medieval village looked like.

SELECT BIBLIOGRAPHY

Bowen, H. C. *Ancient Fields* (1961).
Cantor, L. M. and Wilson, J. D. 'The Medieval Deer Parks of
 Dorset', *Dorset Procs.,* Vol. 83 (1962)—Vol. 90 (1969).
Darby, H. C. and Finn, R. W. *The Domesday Geography of South-
 West England* (1967).
Fagërsten, A. *The Place Names of Dorset* (1933).
R.C.H.M. *Dorset.*
Taylor, C. C. 'Strip-Lynchets', *Antiquity,* Vol. 40 (1966).
Taylor, C. C. 'The Pattern of Medieval Settlement in the Forest
 of Blackmoor', *Dorset Procs.,* Vol. 87 (1966).
Victoria County History, *Dorset,* Vol. 3 (1968).

4. The later medieval landscape, 1300-1500

Desertion and shrinkage of villages. Changes in the farming pattern. Buildings in the landscape

BY 1300 THE landscape of Dorset was more extensively occupied, cultivated and grazed than ever before. Nowhere in the county could one stand and view any scene without the imprint of man's work upon it. On the remotest downs or furthest heath, settlements lay close at hand and sheep and cattle grazed near by. Even in the wooded clay areas one was rarely more than a mile away from some farmstead and its fields. And yet man had by no means reached the limits of his capacity in exploiting the landscape. The margins had been reached but not developed. There were still large areas of chalk and limestone hills, of forest and of heath, which were virtually unknown except to the herdsman or shepherd, the huntsman or woodcutter. But though the exploitation of these marginal lands was to continue, changes were about to take place which were to alter the pattern of continuous development of the landscape as revealed up to now.

In many respects the period from 1300 to 1500 is difficult to unravel in terms of the landscape. The changes that occur at this time are still clearly to be seen, but it is not always easy to be certain of the exact reasons for them. This is largely due to the lack of documentation for the period. Unlike the twelfth and thirteenth centuries, where there are a considerable number of useful sources, and the post-medieval period where one is overwhelmed by documentary material, the later fourteenth and the fifteenth centuries are lacking in the type of documents which are useful to the landscape-historian. As a result it is sometimes possible to do no more than point to the changes in the landscape and to offer some, and possibly questionable, explanations for them.

Desertion and shrinkage of villages

The most marked effect on the landscape of Dorset in the fourteenth to fifteenth centuries was the abandonment and contraction of many of the existing settlements. But it is important to note that this feature was not confined to, or even mainly concerned with, the newest and more isolated settlements in areas of heavy soil or remote parts. Desertion and shrinkage of settlements occurred in the oldest nucleated villages, especially in the chalk regions of the county (Fig. 14). Thus in settlement terms one cannot in Dorset use the description of this period so apt elsewhere, "the retreat from the marginal lands."

There were indeed a few isolated farms that disappeared during this period. A good example may be seen in Sturminster Newton, in the vale of Blackmoor where, on low-lying ground on the south side of the river Stour, are the earthwork remains of a small farmstead. They cover some five acres and consist of five paddocks or enclosures bounded by low banks, with the site of a former house in one of them. This farm, once known as Colber, was already in existence by 1086 but appears to have been deserted soon after the middle of the fourteenth century. Yet, interesting as it is, it is the only deserted medieval farmstead that has been found in the whole of the vale of Blackmoor. Others may exist or have existed, but it is unlikely that there were ever many of them. Examples can occasionally be found elsewhere in the county but they are extremely rare. Only

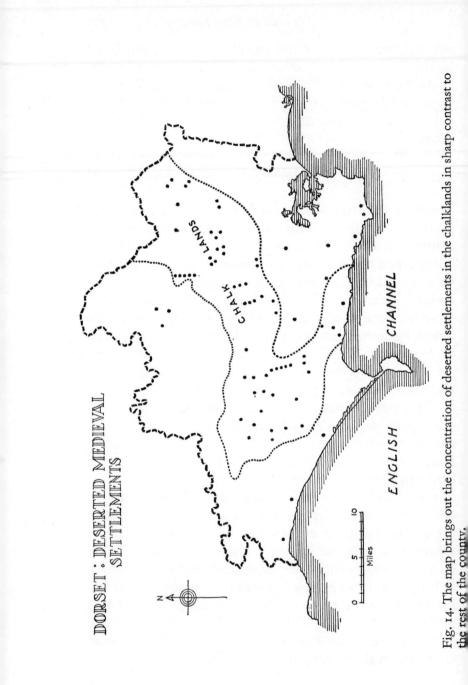

Fig. 14. The map brings out the concentration of deserted settlements in the chalklands in sharp contrast to the rest of the county.

one, in Bloxworth parish, has been noted for the whole of the south Dorset heathland. This is in sharp contrast to the countless farms of early medieval date which still remain. Certainly the great majority of these isolated farms within the forests and heathlands continued to exist throughout this period. There is even evidence of still more new settlements here at this time. At Pulham for example, there is a record of four new 'tenements' being built on the waste of the parish in the late fourteenth century,[1] and it is likely that some of the remote heathland farms, not recorded in documents until the early fifteenth century, may actually date from this time.

Far more important is the evidence of large-scale desertion and shrinkage of the older nucleated settlements. This is also comparatively rare outside the chalklands. The villages of Stock Gaylard, now in Lydlynch parish, and Thorton, now in Marnhull parish, both finally abandoned in the fifteenth century, are amongst the very few examples.

In the chalklands the picture is very different. Not only have whole villages been abandoned or reduced to a hamlet or single farm, but sometimes whole lines of settlements along the chalk valleys have virtually disappeared. Examples of the former kind are the villages of Holworth, now in Chaldon Herring parish (Plate 17), Ringstead in Osmington parish, Friar Mayne in West Knighton and Hemsworth in Witchampton, all reduced to single farmsteads or houses. Examples of the latter may be seen in the North Winterborne valley where six adjacent villages have been reduced to single farms or hamlets (Fig. 6, p. 57), and at Charminster where seven hamlets have almost completely disappeared (Fig. 15). The sites of such settlements are still to be seen as grass-covered banks, ditches and mounds which are all that remain of former houses, paddocks, gardens and streets. Even more common

---

[1] *Somerset and Dorset Notes and Queries,* Vol. 13, p. 272.

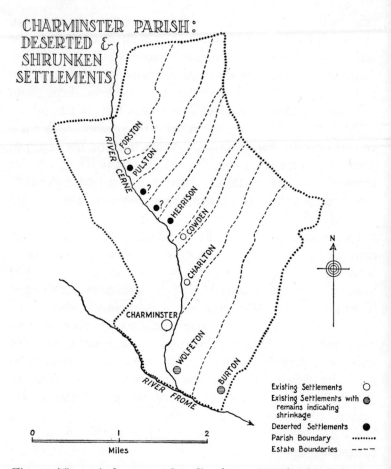

CHARMINSTER PARISH:
DESERTED &
SHRUNKEN
SETTLEMENTS

FORSTON
PULSTON
?
?
HERRISON
COWDEN
CHARLTON
CHARMINSTER
WOLFETON
BURTON

RIVER CERNE

RIVER FROME

N

Existing Settlements ○
Existing Settlements with ◉
remains indicating
shrinkage
Deserted Settlements ●
Parish Boundary ··········
Estate Boundaries ─ ─ ─

0   1   2

Miles

Fig. 15. The typical pattern of medieval estates, each with their associated settlements, here all within a large 'minster parish', is shown on
this map. Almost all of the deserted settlements were apparently
abandoned in the fourteenth and fifteenth centuries. Even the names of
two of them are unknown but their remains still exist on the ground.

than the complete or near-complete desertion is the evidence of major shrinkage in villages in the form of abandoned house sites scattered between the existing buildings. Most of the villages in the Tarrant valley are of this nature, and it is also particularly well illustrated in places such as Farnham and Long Crichel in the north-east.

However, while it is clear that most of this desertion and shrinkage had taken place by the early sixteenth century, it is often difficult to date it accurately. Indeed part of the problem is that the desertion did not apparently occur suddenly but was part of a long-drawn-out process started, assisted or completed by a number of factors. It is also important to realise that the villages that were deserted or shrank in size were those that had always been small. The larger villages rarely appear to have been affected. This may be seen along the middle Piddle valley from Piddlehinton in the north to Burleston in the south-east. While Piddlehinton and Puddletown, which were large settlements even in 1086, still exist today as sizeable villages, all the other settlements in the valley, Little Piddle, Combe Deverall, Muston, North and South Louvard, Waterston, Druce, Bardolfston and Burleston, have either disappeared entirely, or been reduced to a single house or farm. Some detailed examples will make this clearer.

In the Iwerne valley at the north-east end of Stourpaine parish is the site of the former village of Lazerton. It is one of a line of chalkland settlements, each with its own land unit, stretching from Iwerne Minster in the north through Preston, Iwerne Courtney, Ranston, Steepleton, Lazerton and Ash to Stourpaine in the south. Only Iwerne Minster, Iwerne Courtney and Stourpaine remain as villages today. The rest are reduced to single houses or farms. It is certain that the village of Lazerton was virtually deserted by the mid-fifteenth century, for it was not taxed in 1428 because it had fewer than ten inhabitants, and in 1431 the parish of Lazerton was joined to that of Stourpaine because "the church of Lazerton had so small profits that it had been and was then destitute of a chaplain." But even in 1086 it had a recorded population of only seven, that is certainly less than thirty inhabitants, and in the late twelfth century a charter stated that its church was so poor that it was released "from all payments except synodals."

A similar picture can be seen at the former village of Little Piddle, south of Piddlehinton, where there are extensive remains of the former settlement. It had a recorded population of nineteen in 1086, quite a reasonably-sized village by Dorset standards. By about 1290 fifteen householders are recorded and by 1333 only seven taxable householders remained.[2] By 1539 the two recorded households probably occupied the sites of the two existing houses there. At Winterborne Clenston where, as was noted in Chapter 2, there were by the eleventh century three separate villages of Philipston, Clenston and Nicholston, each with its own land unit, the present scattered houses in the parish are linked together by an almost continuous line of earthworks marking the extent of the former villages. The recorded population of these three villages combined was twenty in 1086, but by 1333 only twelve taxable householders are listed. In 1336 the parishes of Clenston (including Philipston) and Nicholston were amalgamated and in 1428 all three villages were exempted from tax as they had fewer than ten inhabitants between them. Thereafter documents record only two or three households there.

These examples can be repeated again and again in the chalklands of Dorset. Even where documentary evidence of desertion is not forthcoming, archaeological evidence helps out. Round Hewish Farm, south of Milton Abbas, earth-work-remains once indicated the former existence of a

---

[2] But see p. 87 for a possible qualification to this statement in general.

village there. Though there is no documentary evidence for its abandonment, destruction of the remains by ploughing in 1965 produced pottery which indicated that while parts of it were abandoned in the early fourteenth century, some occupation went on until the late fourteenth or early fifteenth centuries.

These then are the facts of this curious contraction of settlement mainly in the chalk areas, apparently occurring in the fourteenth and fifteenth centuries. But what are the causes of this desertion and shrinkage? First there can be little doubt that plague played a considerable part, not always a dramatic blow but more often a long-drawn-out process of a dwindling population. Though it is now realised that the Black Death of 1348–50 was not solely responsible for the desertion of all the lost medieval villages of England, there are special reasons for believing that it may have played an important part in Dorset. It was through Dorset that the bubonic plague reached this country, entering by the port of Melcombe Regis almost certainly at the end of June 1348, and there is no doubt that the county was seriously affected by it. A good indication of its severity and distribution can be gathered from the records of the institutions of clergy for late 1348 and 1349.[3] At Winterborne Clenston four new rectors were instituted and at nearby Winterborne Houghton three new incumbents were appointed during this period. At many other places two or more new incumbents are instituted in a short time and the total number of institutions for the whole county is exceptionally large. If we assume that the distribution of such new incumbents shows where the plague was most severe some interesting implications emerge. While there are a large number of institutions in villages along the coast which one might expect, in general the chalk areas of the county have far more new clergy

[3] Sarum Epis. Reg., Wyville, II, ff. 90–191.

than other parts. Too much weight must not be placed on this evidence. The distribution of deserted and shrunken settlements does not exactly match that of mortality among the clergy, but at least it suggests that there might be a connection between the final desertion of some of the already small settlements in the chalklands and the plague which appears to have affected this same region more than any other part of the county. Perhaps the constricted nature of many of the chalkland settlements aided the spread of the plague among these communities. Other factors also certainly played a part in this contraction of settlement. The plague returned again and again, and indeed became endemic in England for some 300 years. The year 1381 is known to have been an exceptionally bad one in Dorset but little is recorded of its detailed effects. It is also possible that the thin chalk soils were losing their fertility after some 4000 years of cultivation, or that the water-table in the chalk was falling as a result of the continued clearance of lower, heavier land. The general and well-known economic decline of the period must also have played a part, and, as will be seen later, there was certainly a reduction in arable land and an increase in pasture at this time. At present, however, we cannot satisfactorily explain the decline of chalkland settlements in this period but it probably involved a combination of the factors put forward above and possibly others. It must remain an unexplained mystery of the Dorset landscape.

Changes in the farming pattern

In addition to the contraction of settlement there were also important changes in the farming scene. Some of these were county-wide, but others show a marked difference between the chalk and non-chalk areas. On the chalklands the shrinkage and desertion of settlements was accompanied by a large-scale reduction in the amount of arable land. The arable fields on the high downland, broken up in the twelfth and thirteenth centuries, were abandoned in the late medieval period and the downs reverted to grassland, leaving only the slight undulations of ridge and furrow to show us today where the earlier farmers ploughed. Further, many of the permanent common-fields on the lower land in the chalk valleys seem to have been largely enclosed in the fourteenth and fifteenth centuries, though dating is difficult and it is impossible to say whether they were enclosed piecemeal or all at once. But the common-fields which do disappear are, in the main, those belonging to very small villages or to settlements which were deserted or much reduced in size at this time. In the larger villages where there was no marked reduction in population, the common-fields remained in existence. At Ranston in the Iwerne valley, the common-fields occupied a large area of the parish in 1274, but had disappeared completely by the late fifteenth century. They were probably enclosed at the time when the village was abandoned, perhaps in the early fifteenth century. Similarly, while there was still a three-field system in operation at Winterborne Clenston in 1315, this had been completely enclosed 200 years later and the village was finally deserted by the mid-fifteenth century.

This abandonment of arable land on the chalk was matched by an increase in sheep farming. Though sheep had always been kept on the downs, often in considerable numbers, the fourteenth century saw the appearance of really large flocks. The numbers of sheep recorded in fourteenth- and fifteenth-century documents were not high by later standards, but they now became increasingly common. Even by 1330 there were over 1000 sheep on the demesne land alone of the estate of Glastonbury Abbey at Buckland Newton[4] and in 1329–3 there is a record of

[4] Keil, 'Farming on the Dorset Estates of Glastonbury Abbey', *Dorset Procs.*, Vol. 87 (1966).

7000 sheep on the various manors of Bindon Abbey. At Tarrant Launceston in 1397 400 sheep were kept by the lord of the manor quite apart from an unknown number belonging to twenty-seven tenants. In 1364 a staple was established at the port of Melcombe Regis to deal with the increasing export of wool from the county. National records of the late fourteenth and early fifteenth centuries continually expressed concern at the amount of wool produced in the county which was being made into cloth both in Dorset and in adjoining areas and thus reducing crown revenue on direct wool exports. During the latter part of the fifteenth century the numbers of sheep in the county continued to rise and trade in both wool and cloth increased.

Outside the chalk regions both similar and different changes were taking place. As on the chalk, common-fields were being enclosed during this period, though here it was certainly not always associated with deserted settlements, which in any case were rare in these areas. In the vale of Blackmoor, at Purse Caundle, the common-fields disappeared in the early fifteenth century, at Marnhull between 1361 and 1410 and at Hazelbury Bryan by 1434, certainly in the latter case to be replaced by large enclosed fields of permanent pasture. Similar evidence exists for places such as Symondsbury in the west of the county and Woodsford in the south Dorset heathland, as well as for many others.

Yet this enclosure was not the result of the contraction of agriculture. The clearing or assarting of the waste and forests went on uninterrupted. In a document of 1412 concerning the land held in Dorset by Cirencester Abbey, it is related that about 1376 "a former abbot . . . appropriated to himself and his house three hundred acres of pasture . . . which belonged to his manor of West Pulham", and that the abbey "hold and occupy these three hundred acres enclosed by themselves . . . in severalty still." Even the small peasant continued to make encroachments on the

Plate 16 Barnston Manor, Church Knowle. One of the few surviving medieval manor houses in the county. Dating from the thirteenth century, it still retains its original hall. It is constructed of the local Purbeck limestone.

Plate 17 The deserted village of Holworth, Chaldon Herring. A superb example of its kind. The

Plate 18 Bradford Abbas church. One of the best examples of the remarkable series of fifteenth-century church towers in the county. Most of this church was rebuilt in the mid-fifteenth century.

Plate 19 Athelhampton Hall. Though much altered, the greater part of the house, built by Sir William Martyn in the late fifteenth century with money gained [...] commerce and trade in London, still remains

waste, as at Stoke Wake in 1390 when "Edmund Sycock appropriated and enclosed a piece of the King's land ten perches long and seven feet wide and worth one penny yearly."[5]

Many of the medieval deer parks were also converted to other uses. Knighton Park in Canford on the heath in the east of the county was disparked in 1462 and leased out for pasture, while that at Wynford Eagle had been divided into pasture closes by the sixteenth century.

This then is the picture of settlement and agriculture between 1300 and the late fifteenth century. Though the details are sometimes blurred there is evidence of disease and pestilence, abandonment of settlement and fields and of a general economic decline. All this seems to have resulted in much poverty and hardship, and this is emphasised by the fact that in 1435 and again in 1449 as many as 137 villages and hamlets, scattered fairly evenly over the whole county, asked for, and received, a reduction in taxation on account of poverty. Yet the picture is not entirely black. Though it is true that for most people and especially the lower classes these years were dark ones, there is in the present landscape clear evidence that for some these years were good ones, marked by a certain prosperity. This evidence lies in the buildings of the fourteenth and fifteenth centuries to which we must now turn.

Buildings in the landscape

In sharp contrast to the apparent decline and poverty of this period, as already described, the contemporary buildings of Dorset reflect great prosperity. The most marked feature of this wealth is to be seen in the churches of the county. During the late fourteenth and fifteenth centuries most

5 'Calendar of Miscellaneous Inquisitions for 1390'; *Somerset and Dorset Notes and Queries,* Vol. 13, p. 272.

Dorset churches underwent alteration. Many were enlarged or entirely rebuilt, but most characteristic was the addition of great west towers in the Perpendicular style, many of considerable beauty. By comparison with other parts of the country this Perpendicular work is sometimes plain and the detail of lower quality but the overall picture is impressive. In the north and west the new towers were built to a fairly standard pattern using Ham Hill stone from the quarries not far away in Somerset, but exceptionally fine ones exist at Beaminster, Whitchurch Canonicorum and Bradford Abbas (Plate 18). In the centre of the county the local limestone and greensand were used in the construction of a fine group of towers of which Okeford Fitzpaine and Durweston are amongst the best. In the south-east the quarries in Purbeck and Portland provided the stone for a similar series of towers.

But fine buildings of this period are not confined to churches though naturally these have survived later vicissitudes more readily than other buildings. There was an increase in the numbers of good houses built not only by the greater landlords but by the rising class of yeoman farmers. And it was often these people who paid for the great church rebuilding.

Who were these people? Many were long-established Dorset families such as the Binghams who had lived at Binghams Melcombe since the thirteenth century, gradually enlarging their estates, and growing wealthy. Almost nothing remains of their original home because of later rebuilding, but it was in the fourteenth and fifteenth centuries that they founded the fortunes of their line. They were certainly responsible for the almost complete rebuilding, during the mid-fourteenth century, of the parish church which still stands a short distance from the house.

The Martyns of Athelhampton are another old Dorset family who grew prosperous at this period. They had for long lived at Waterston near Puddletown, but in the four-teenth century they moved further down the river Piddle to Athelhampton from whence they supervised their exten-sive estates. However, this family looked beyond the county for its wealth and by the fifteenth century had moved into commerce. Its most distinguished member, Sir William Martyn, was lord mayor of London in 1493, and as well as extensive commercial interests, also held the lucrative office of Collector of Tonnage and Poundage in the City. It was Sir William who began the building of the present Athelhampton Hall in the late fifteenth century (Plate 19). Though now only a fragment of its former magnificence, the great open hall, with its fine timber roof and oriel window, is the work of Sir William Martyn. The family, like the Binghams, also glorified their local church at Puddletown. They appear to have been largely responsible for a continuous rebuilding of this church from the late fourteenth century to the early sixteenth. It included a fine tower completed in the late fifteenth century, perhaps at the expense of Sir William himself, and a superb south chapel dated to 1460 in which many of the family are buried.

Another family which has left substantial remains of its wealth at a slightly earlier date is the Latimer family. This again was an old county line which for long occupied Duntish manor near Buckland Newton. Around 1335 William Latimer, a younger son, married a rich heiress through whom he obtained the manor of Fiddleford at Sturminster Newton. As well as being a substantial land-owner, Latimer, like Sir William Martyn, had outside sources of income, though in this case it was the crown which pro-vided it. Latimer was Subsidy Commissioner for Dorset in 1371 and Sheriff of Somerset and Dorset in 1374 and 1380. There is no doubt that the late fourteenth-century great hall with its splendid and elaborately carved roof that still remains at Fiddleford was built by him.

Great wealth, however, was not confined to old Dorset families. New people also came into the county with new sources of wealth and these too left their mark on the landscape. In 1428 one Richard Long paid 100 marks of silver for 575 acres of land in Purse Caundle. Long was a relative of a family in South Wraxall in Wiltshire who were wealthy clothiers. It was this Richard Long who built Purse Caundle manor house in the centre of his new estate. It then consisted of a large open hall with cross-wings of normal late medieval plan, together with a beautiful oriel window in the hall, and a fine porch leading into the screens passage. Though the house has been subsequently much altered and added to, the original hall remains open to the roof, as in Richard Long's day.

Here again, Long and his descendants glorified their local church. Purse Caundle church was entirely rebuilt during the fifteenth century and though largely rebuilt later still retains its west tower and chancel arch which, more than the tombs inside, stand as a monument to the Long family. Not all wealthy families managed to survive the economic troubles of the time. The Longs, Martyns, Latimers and Binghams all achieved wealth by, as far as we can see, moving into the textile industry as farmers, traders or clothiers. But to move into an expanding industry was not enough. Judicious marriages with suitable heiresses as William Latimer achieved were also important. And astute and perhaps ruthless estate management counted for much. It is probably not without significance that the common-fields of Purse Caundle were enclosed when the Longs lived there, and that the village of Binghams Melcombe disappeared in the early fifteenth century.

This increased wealth was not confined only to the upper and merchant classes, though naturally it is these people who are best documented. It is also reflected in the rise of a new class of yeoman-farmers which also started at this time. Little is known of them and only a few of their farms have survived later rebuilding. One such is Naish Farm in Holwell parish which is situated just beyond the outer edge of the common-fields of the village in an area of irregular enclosed fields cut out of the waste before the thirteenth century. Externally at least it is quite unimpressive. Inside, however, is a remarkably complete fifteenth-century yeoman-farmer's house with a room arrangement imitating the contemporary great houses. There is a small hall only twelve feet by seventeen feet once open to the roof, an undercroft with a solar above at one end and, beyond a screens passage, a kitchen at the other. This is the best surviving example of a handful of similar houses which are all that survive of the homes of these new farmers. They represent the visible wealth of the more successful peasants, who took advantage of the economic situation of the late fourteenth and early fifteenth centuries and leased at low rents land being offered by the greater landlords in financial difficulties. This rise of a new farming class marks the beginning of immense social and economic changes which were to come to full flood in the sixteenth and seventeenth centuries and which were to have profound effects on the landscape.

SELECT BIBLIOGRAPHY

R.C.H.M. *Dorset*.
Taylor, C. C. 'Lost Dorset Place-Names', *Dorset Procs.*, Vol. 88 (1967).
Victoria County History. *Dorset,* Vol. 2 (1908).

5. Tudor to Early Georgian Dorset

Changes in the farming scene. New buildings

BETWEEN THE LATE fifteenth and the mid-eighteenth centuries the rural landscape of Dorset began to take on its present appearance as a result of profound social and economic changes. Some of these had been in progress for many centuries or had at least started long ago, but other forces now combined with them to speed up the development of the landscape. There is no shortage of evidence, either visual or documentary, to trace these changes, and here we can pick out only the most important.

For most of the generations under review there was a general economic expansion, which enabled farming in particular to prosper and to become increasingly specialised. In addition, commercial expansion on a countywide scale brought new wealth to a large number of people. Almost all classes of society benefited and the period was one of great social movement with increased standards of living for many. As a result of the break-up of the monastic estates from the 1540s onwards, there occurred the greatest transfer of land since the Norman Conquest. Yeoman-farmers, whose forebears had leased the land they worked, now purchased it and often as the result of careful management rose higher in the social scale. The upper classes themselves became more mobile and were further reinforced by a considerable influx of men who had made fortunes in commerce. New ideas, tastes and standards from elsewhere in England and from the continent permeated the upper half of society. Advances in living conditions and in agricultural techniques and new fashions in architecture and garden design swept over the country in an ever increasing flood. All stamped their mark upon the landscape.

Changes in the farming scene

The most marked aspect of the Dorset landscape from the sixteenth century onwards, noted by all contemporary writers, was the vast flocks of sheep which occupied large parts of the county. Leland in the 1540s speaks of the chalk lands north of the river Frome as having "little corn and no wood, but all about great flokkes of sheppe"; Camden in 1586 wrote that these same downs "feed flocks of sheepe in great numbers" and Thomas Gerard writing in 1633 said that the downs were "all overspread with inumerable Flockes of Sheepe." Edward Leigh wrote in 1659 that there were "within six miles of Dorchester three hundred thousand sheep" and by 1724 Defoe claimed that there were 600,000 in the same area. Both these latter figures are probably exaggerated, but there can be no doubt that large and increasing numbers of sheep were kept on the downs in this period. Local documents give us detailed and perhaps more accurate figures for specific places. Sir Roger Newburgh of East Lulworth, who died in 1515, left 4,000 sheep on his land, and in 1550 at least 2,700 sheep were kept on a single farm in Sydling St Nicholas. In 1753 a farmer at Hilton, one John White, with very little land owned over 500 sheep but had only thirty-three cattle and six pigs.

These large flocks of sheep were made possible only by specialisation and the introduction of new techniques which are still reflected in the present landscape. One of these was the enclosure of large areas of former open downland into large, generally rectangular fields, not only for the better control of feeding and breeding of sheep but also for the introduction of new crop rotations at this time.

Dorset

Often such enclosures were carried out by agreement between all the parties concerned. At Long Bredy shortly before 1597 the lord of the manor and his tenants agreed to enclose "a good part of the commons and waste ground of the manor" specifically for sheep. Around 1620 three major landowners agreed to divide and enclose much of the downland in the adjacent parishes of Hooke, North Poorton and Toller Porcorum, north-west of Dorchester. In 1716 all the downland at Blandford St Mary, and in 1741 all the downland at Bradford Peverell was enclosed by agreement. These enclosures may still be seen today, in the form of large, somewhat irregular fields bounded by quick-set hedges on low banks. In other cases attempts at enclosure by the lord of the manor alone were opposed by tenants who rightly feared a loss of their common rights on the open downs. In the early sixteenth century two separate suits were brought in the Court of the Star Chamber by the tenants of Sir William Fyloll in Bincombe and Winterborne Came, in an attempt to stop him enclosing the common downland for sheep. Unfortunately the result is not known.

In many other places on the downs, though the process is undocumented, the present landscape shows that it went on. High on the downland, east of the village of Piddletrenthide, and beyond the area of its former common-fields, is an extensive tract of land covering some 400 acres, divided into a number of large sub-rectangular fields up to twenty-five acres in extent, with two much larger areas of seventy to eighty acres each. In the centre of this region is Dole's Ash Farm, a building which dates from the seventeenth century. It seems likely that the whole area was enclosed for sheep at that time. Even outside the chalklands on the sandstone and limestone hills in the west there is evidence of enclosure at this period. For example, in 1677 all the land on Blackdown Hill at Broadwindsor was enclosed by agreement.

The importance of sheep at this time must not, however, allow us to make the mistake of believing that all these downland enclosures were only for these animals. This period was also one of great improvement on the arable side of farming. New land was being enclosed specifically for new crops which were being introduced. While Dr Kerridge's assertion that from the 1560s to 1720 "the plough was making more or less continual inroads into the downlands" may not be strictly accurate for Dorset at least, there can be no doubt that large amounts of downland were being enclosed and ploughed at this time. But the total was probably not very great compared with the late eighteenth- and nineteenth-century enclosures.[1]

The enclosure of downland was also accompanied by enclosure of common-fields, often, but not always, connected with sheep farming. The suits against Sir William Fyloll noted above, were not only concerned with the enclosure of the downland but also with the threat to convert the arable land in the parishes to sheep pastures. In 1548 the common-fields of Iwerne Courtney were completely enclosed following an agreement between the lord of the manor and his tenants. There was a careful and equal redistribution of the land involved so that each person's allotment could be conveniently hedged and farmed in severalty. Though many of these hedges have disappeared, it is possible to see the various sizes of the enclosures in some of the present fields which still have C or reversed-S curves in their hedge-lines indicating the former strips and furlongs which were fenced.

On the other hand an attempt by the lord of a manor in Charminster, one William Harlyn, to enclose his parts of the common-fields there in 1577 led to a dispute with some of his tenants. The resulting agreement and redistribution of land was carefully arranged so that Harlyn and some tenants were enabled to enclose their land while others continued

[1] Kerridge, *The Agricultural Revolution* (1967).

to work their land in the old way for another 250 years. This partial enclosure of common-fields occurred frequently all over Dorset at this time and many parishes show evidence of slow piecemeal enclosure of this type. At Hinton St Mary, by the late sixteenth century, almost half the original common-fields appear to have been enclosed, mainly for pasture and while some of the tenants occupied enclosed land only, most had at least half their land in the remaining common arable fields. These enclosures can still be seen south of the village where the modern fields consist of long, narrow, curved plots, formerly groups of individual strips. Similarly a mid-seventeenth-century perambulation of Gillingham in the north of the county specifically mentions new enclosures in the common-fields in the following way: "Out into Magstone Field [one of the common-fields] into a ground newly enclosed by Mr Barnes . . ."[2] Mr Barnes' field can still be seen today, easily recognisable by its long strip-like shape, lying in an area of much later rectangular fields.

The increased area of pasture and its division into fields certainly allowed more sheep to be kept. But other sources were needed as well. Particularly important were spring pastures where sheep could be grazed when the upland pastures were not suitable. One way of obtaining this was to enclose the old common meadows near the streams and for this there is plenty of evidence. In 1687 Nicholas Gould leased "a piece of ground lately fenced in out of a meadow" to Thomas Wood, shearsman, at Broadway. These have now disappeared but the "newly enclosed meadow" in Kington Magna, which was sold in 1699 by Samuel Ryall who is termed a clothier, still exists on the edge of the river Cale divided into small rectangular fields.

For those with capital and suitable land, the best way of improving meadows from the seventeenth century

[2] *Somerset and Dorset Notes and Queries,* Vol. 17, p. 80.

onwards, to provide good feed for sheep when it was most needed, was to construct water-meadows in the river valleys. This complex process involved the building of a network of artificial channels designed to distribute river water over the alluvial pastures and drain it off again (Plate 20) The river would be dammed and a 'Head Main' constructed to carry the water to a complicated series of 'water carriages' or long ridges which had drains or channels down their spines. So during the 'floating' of these water-meadows the aim was to have a continuous movement of water along the brimful channels in the ridges which spilt over and ran down their sides into the intervening furrows and so back into the rivers. By floating these meadows during the winter early frost-free pasture was obtained and sheep were turned out on to them usually between February and May when pasture elsewhere was lacking or in short supply. The development and use of water-meadows during the seventeenth and more particularly in the eighteenth and nineteenth centuries played a vital part in the agricultural economy for they allowed far more sheep to be kept than would otherwise have been possible. The earliest documented reference to water-meadows in the county is in 1629 at Puddletown. In the manor court after "a great debate beinge theare had and questions moved by some of the tenants about wateringe and improvinge theire grounds" it was agreed to begin construction of water-meadows. Further meadows were laid out here in 1636 and an agreement made in 1635 for 'floating' the common meadows in Winfrith Newburgh had been implemented by 1658. In Moreton and Bovingdon the demesne meadows had been 'floated' before 1649.[3] By the mid-eighteenth century water meadows were common in the south and central parts of the county. Though now no longer used, the remains of these water-meadows, with their ridges, channels, drains and

[3] Kerridge, *op. cit.*, pp. 251–67.

elaborate sluices, are still a marked feature of large areas of the valley floors of the rivers Frome and Piddle, and are also common in many of the smaller chalkland and heathland valleys.

In the clay lands of the county there was also a marked agricultural expansion in this period which is still visible in the landscape. Sheep played a part here too, for they were often brought down into these areas during the winter. There were also a number of specialised crops grown which led to an increase in arable land. But the main specialisation here was cattle. Thomas Gerard in 1633 noted that these areas abounded in "verie good Pastures and Feedings for cattell."

In terms of the landscape, this agricultural development continued the long established process of clearing and enclosing the forest and waste, though it was very often on a large scale. One of the largest was the almost total enclosure of Gillingham Forest in the north of the county in the early seventeenth century. The royal forest there remained largely unenclosed until 1624 when it was finally disafforested. During the next two decades much of the forest was enclosed. An area of some 5,000 acres was cleared, divided into characteristically large fields and a whole series of isolated farms built there. Both farms and fields remain today and provide a landscape markedly different from that of the smaller, irregular fields around them which date from a much earlier period. These enclosures gave rise to serious riots both in 1624 and later in 1642–5 as local people objected to the loss of their common rights. Elsewhere, however, similar enclosures were made peacefully by agreement between all parties as at Hilfield in 1697–8. Here the whole of the common land of the parish covering some 300 acres was broken up into large sub-rectangular fields which still remain there today.

Many other places show evidence of assarting or enclosure on a smaller scale. In Lydlynch parish, in the heart of the Blackmoor Vale, this period saw piecemeal enclosure of the large areas of waste still remaining. Part of Haydon Common was divided into fields and an isolated farmstead built among them in the late sixteenth century to judge from the date of the present farmhouse. Later in another part of the parish the former Rodmore Common, some 200 acres in all, was cleared, broken up into fields of markedly geometric shapes and the present Little Rodmore Farm built sometime in the early eighteenth century. Not far away a small area of common woodland, known as Beaulieu Common, lying across the boundaries of Pulham and Buckland Newton parishes, was enclosed by agreement between the landowners of both parishes in 1700 and 1724.

Not even the remote infertile heathlands were immune to enclosure at this period. The report of a Commission of Enquiry into the state of Holt Forest in east Dorset for the Duchy of Lancaster in 1598 shows this well. In it there is a note that "there is adjoining to the park pale a little plott of grounde conteyninge aboute an acre at a place called Croked Wythes inclosed by one Thomas Charter . . . uppon which is erected a cottage . . . which is verie inconvenient, as well for the spoyling of the deare as for spoyling the woods and otherwise." Inconvenient or not the enclosure remained and still stands today with its cottage at Crooked Withies on the north-eastern edge of Holt Heath.

At the same time the great landlords carried out reclamation of heathland on an enormous scale for both sheep and arable. The same 1598 Enquiry also records that Sir Matthew Arundel of Hampreston had enclosed some 200 acres of Holt Heath and that Mr John Avery of Uddens House had claimed 400 acres of the heath and had been molesting the Queen's tenants who had turf-cutting rights there. Later on in the early seventeenth century Sir John Banks of Kingston Lacey enclosed 400 acres of the heath.

All these enclosures are still clearly visible today. Many of the fields round the edges of the heath are of this date and the remains of others which were not so permanent are visible as low banks whenever the gorse and bracken are burnt off.

One particularly curious form of enclosure on the heathland occurred in 1633 in West Parley parish in the extreme east of the county. In 1575 the lord of the manor there had sold all his land to the tenants. The large area of heathland there, the 'great Wastes', remained open and by 1619 disputes had broken out amongst these tenants over whether to enclose it or not. The case went to the Court of Chancery which decided in favour of the enclosers. A Commission was set up to undertake the enclosure and in order that all the interested parties received an absolutely fair allotment of the variable heathland they were given long narrow strips of land extending right across the parish. Thus one John Bolton received an allotment of fifteen acres which was twenty-two yards wide and nearly two miles long! These curious allotments were never in fact entirely cultivated and were used mainly for pasture and turf-cutting. The low banks dividing them can still be seen today stretching endlessly across West Parley Heath.

The ultimate project in this period of agricultural expansion was a far-fetched and ill-considered scheme to drain the Fleet, the area of sea lying between Chesil Beach and the mainland west of Weymouth. This is a long narrow lagoon some eight miles long and between 100 yards and half a mile wide. The attempt to drain it was made by Sir George Horsey and others between 1630 and 1646. The legal arrangements, the fact that the organisers called themselves Adventurers, and some of the technical details, recall the contemporary draining of the Fenlands of Eastern England and was perhaps suggested by these works. However, the Dorset venture was a complete failure and though a great deal of money and labour was poured into a 'great Dam' and 'divers sluices of stone and Tymber... howbeit by some accident and likewise by reason of Stormy windes and tempests the Sea did force or cast upp much Sea Water over and through the gravelly or sandy bank" (i.e. Chesil Beach).

In this account of the agricultural changes in this period there has been little mention of the people involved in it, who they were, and how they made their wealth. It is now time to look at them and this we may do through the buildings which they have left in the landscape.

New buildings

During the long period from 1500 to 1750 a vast amount of building and rebuilding by all classes of society took place. The remains of this activity illustrate vividly the wealth, status and aspirations of the builders and an examination of these people and their houses will put into correct perspective the changes and developments in the contemporary agricultural landscape. The most important developments were carried out by the larger landowners and it is these at which we must first look.

The early sixteenth century saw the end of the great monastic houses, but before they disappeared some of them had a brief, but remarkable, architectural flowering. In the last fifty years or so of their existence, fine new buildings appeared at some of these establishments. Perhaps the best known is the porch to the Abbot's Hall at Cerne Abbey. The Hall was built by Abbot Thomas Sam (1497–1509) and the porch is a superb example of early sixteenth-century workmanship. More impressive is the rebuilding at Forde Abbey, Thorncombe, by the last abbot, Thomas Charde (1521–39). This included a splendid new abbot's lodging and part of the cloister. At Milton Abbas, Abbot

William Middleton erected in 1498 the magnificent Great Hall which still stands. These works reflect great wealth which certainly came in all three cases from the vast flocks of sheep possessed by these houses. However, they probably reflect also an attempt by these houses to dispose of some surplus capital before the crown could lay hands on it, though presumably none of the builders ever thought that Henry VIII would take the final step to end their existence.

Turning now to the more important secular landlords, the whole period was one of great social change and movement. A statistical study of great Dorset landlords in the early seventeenth century shows this well. Of 211 leading Dorset families in 1634 nearly half appear for the first time between 1529 and 1603. Part of this was produced by a remarkable immigration into the county of small farmers and gentry, especially from Devon at this time. But even within the county itself there were many yeomen who, as Thomas Gerard wrote in 1633, "now beginne to encroach upon the Gentrie." One such was the Strode family of Parnham near Beaminster. Their rise from small farmers began in the fifteenth century by careful land management and astute purchases, but was greatly helped by a marriage to an heiress of the Parnham estate. Then in 1522 Robert Strode of Parnham married Elizabeth, granddaughter of Sir William Hardy, Chief Baron of the Exchequer under Henry VII, and it was probably the resulting increase in his fortunes that enabled him to rebuild his father's house at Parnham some years later when he succeeded to the estate. The fine house there, though much altered, still retains its great hall and one cross-wing of this rebuilding. The family continued to extend their estates and in 1612 rebuilt Chantmarle House, Cattistock, following the purchase of the manor there in 1604.

Many other houses of this period also reflect the changing social order. Their builders had very varied origins. Some

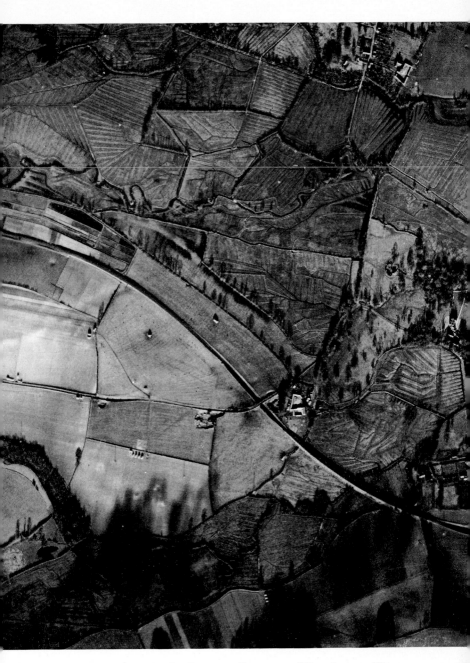

Plate 20 Water-meadows in the Frome valley, east of Dorchester. The complexity of a broad river valley completely filled with fully developed water-meadows can only be appreciated from the air.

Plate 21 Anderson Manor. Built in 1622. One of the earliest brick houses in Dorset, though for its date designed in a rather archaic manner on an E-plan.

Plate 22 Hanford House. Built between 1604 and 1623 by Sir Robert Seymer. The central doorway was once the entrance into an open courtyard now roofed over. In contrast to the contemporary Anderson Manor (Plate 21), it is of an extremely advanced design.

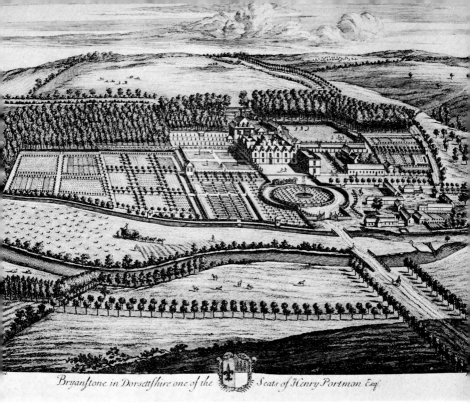

Bryanstone in Dorsettshire one of the Seats of Henry Portman Esq.

Plate 23 Bryanston in the early eighteenth century. The house lay down by the
river Stour, adjacent to the church and surrounded by formal gardens. There
is no real park and the countryside is still close at hand.

Plate 24 Bryanston House today. The last great country house built in Dorset.
Its position on a high hill dominating all around it, its ponderous grandeur
and size contrast with its predecessors and illustrate the final achievement of
Victorian landed aristocracy.

Plate 25 Meerhay Farm, Beaminster. A typical Dorset farm, high up in a remote valley. It was built in 1610 by a local yeoman-farmer. However, judging by its name, the farmstead must be of twelfth- or thirteenth-century origin at least and perhaps much older.

were old established families, others were newly rich merchants and lawyers, but many came to Dorset with little except their ability and industry to back them. Some failed, and of these we know almost nothing, but others succeeded and as they advanced in wealth through trade, the law, or crown appointments, they acquired pedigrees, houses and estates. The latter were often ruthlessly exploited and improved to continue the increase in the family fortunes.

The dissolution of the monastic houses brought in a number of new families to Dorset of which the Tregonwells is one of the most interesting. John Tregonwell, one of the Commissioners for the surrender of monasteries in Dorset, bought the site and much of the land of Milton Abbey. He was a lawyer, and a member of an old Cornish family, who made his mark as one of the Proctors in Henry VIII's divorce case, for which he was knighted. He moved to Milton and soon made considerable alterations there though these no longer exist. The family continued to improve and enlarge its estates and a later John Tregonwell built the extremely fine house at Anderson near Bere Regis in 1622 (Plate 21). Though its design, an E-shaped plan with a three-gabled symmetrical composition, was old-fashioned by the early seventeenth century, it had a sophisticated room arrangement for its time and more important it was built in brick, a material then comparatively new in Dorset.

Another family who gained from the dissolution was the Strangways of Melbury Sampford. The family originated in Yorkshire and a branch came to Dorset in 1500, no doubt with an eye to improving its wealth from the ubiquitous sheep. Sir Giles Strangway rebuilt the house at Melbury just before 1540. The plan was in the late medieval tradition with a hall approached across a small courtyard. But over the entrance was built a magnificent tower capped by an hexagonal lantern with a battlemented parapet over it.

This tower, which still remains, is quite unusual. Much of the money for this rebuilding came from the careful management of large estates, not only in the immediate locality, but also in the vale of Blackmoor, which Sir Giles gradually acquired during his lifetime. However, the real wealth of the family came from Sir Giles' position as one of the Commissioners for the surrender of the Dorset monasteries. Thus in 1542 he bought almost all the land of Abbotsbury Abbey. At Melbury he also made the great park to set off his new house, before his death in 1547.

His son improved the family's fortune still more by marriage, and succeeding generations continued to increase their estates. Amongst these, Sir John Strangway, who has been described as one of the shrewdest estate managers in the county in the seventeenth century was typical. When the great estates of the Earls of Suffolk were dispersed, he bought up the splendid sheep pastures of Pulston in Charminster and increased the rents there by fifty per cent. The result of this kind of management may be seen in the house at Melbury, which was extensively altered and enlarged in the late seventeenth century in a severe, but for Dorset, remarkably advanced Classical style.

Another family which managed to achieve great wealth and position through working for the crown was Seymer of Hanford. The family only leased their small estate until 1599 when Sir Robert Seymer bought it. As one of the Tellers of the Exchequer he was well placed to acquire wealth and within a very short time he purchased large estates in the area. His official position enabled him to judge the moment when debts to the crown would force the sale of property and it was by this means that he bought the manor of Stoke Wake from the recusant Keynes. Largely by means of this rapidly accumulated wealth Sir Robert was able to build Hanford House between 1604 and 1623 (Plate 22). The house was planned round a central courtyard, now roofed over, on the model of an Italian Renaissance palace, but suitably adapted for the cold English climate with large windows looking inwards to the courtyard. Its somewhat ponderous grandeur well illustrates the ideals of the affluent in the early seventeenth century.

The greater the position under the crown the more spectacular were the rewards and the subsequent effect on the landscape. Sir John Digby, later Earl of Bristol, who was an ambassador to Spain bought Sherborne New Castle in 1617. The house had been built by another crown servant, Sir Walter Raleigh, around 1595 as a renaissance 'castle' comprising a rectangular central block with four angle turrets. Sir John greatly enlarged this in 1625 by the addition of four wings terminating in hexagonal towers each pair flanking a courtyard on either side of the original house.

Similarly Sir John Banks, Attorney General to Charles I, was able to purchase Corfe Castle in 1635 and was also able to make large additions to his estates including that of Kingston Lacey near Wimborne. In spite of the disastrous times of the Civil War, during which Corfe Castle was reduced to a ruin, his son Sir Ralph Banks was able to build a new family seat at Kingston Lacey in the years 1663–5. This splendid house is one of the earliest examples of Classical architecture in the county. The family continued to prosper and were extremely able estate managers. The work of Sir John himself in reclaiming the wastes of Holt Heath has already been noted and in the family papers there are numerous references to the draining and fertilizing of their estates throughout the seventeenth and eighteenth centuries.

Finally we must look at the merchants, both local and immigrant, who put much of their accumulated wealth into houses and land and often rose rapidly in society. Of local origin was John Henning of Poole who bought an estate at Poxwell, near Dorchester. His son, who rose to become Sheriff of the county in 1609, built Poxwell House, which was described as "fair and new" in 1625. This was no fashionable palace but a long, low house, built on a traditional medieval plan with a great hall, and a delightful mock defensive gatehouse guarding the entrance into the courtyard. Of the immigrant merchants, perhaps the best known is Humphrey Weld. He came from a long line of very wealthy London merchants who already had extensive estates in the home counties when Humphrey Weld bought a large part of the Dorset land of the Earl of Suffolk in 1641 and moved into the fantastic Lulworth Castle. It was a castle in name only and with its towers and battlements has been justly described as being "in accord with Tudor pageantry" and "with an affinity with Spencerian poetry."[4] It had been built between 1588 and 1609 by the second and third Viscount Bindon, though never finished. It was left to Humphrey Weld to complete it, and it says much for his financial status that he did this on a very lavish scale. Even now, empty and gaunt after a disastrous fire, it still remains one of the most remarkable and evocative of all Dorset houses. The Welds too took a great interest in their estates, perhaps because their Catholic religion kept them out of public life. Among the abundant records relating to their lands, probably the splendid collection of detailed eighteenth-century estate maps shows best the careful way in which the family managed land.

This brief look at a few of the sixteenth- and seventeenth-century great houses of Dorset has enabled us to see the origins and aims of some of the people who through their large estates wrought great changes in the rural landscape. Many more examples might be given, for Dorset is exceptionally rich in fine houses of this period. But we must also look at these and other houses in a wider sense to see how

4 R.C.H.M., *Dorset*, Vol. 2.

they reflected the changing fashions in living conditions and designs.

At the beginning of the sixteenth century all the great houses were still conceived in the medieval tradition. That is, all had a great hall, often open to the roof, with a kitchen block or wing at one end and at the other a wing used for private bedrooms and sitting-rooms. We have already noted fifteenth-century examples of this at Purse Caundle and Athelhampton, and others continued to be built during the sixteenth century. These late-medieval houses have a generally rambling appearance, and however attractive, can hardly be said to have been 'designed'.

From the sixteenth century onwards, new ideas of living standards became desirable and new ideas in design fashionable. Perhaps the two most important factors were a growing desire for symmetrical elevations, especially to the front of a building, and a change from one main living-room, the great hall, to a multiplicity of rooms for special purposes. These ideas, combined with a conservative attempt to retain something of the old medieval layout, led to all kinds of complications in room arrangements and, more important from the landscape point of view, to strange appearances which still remain to show the owner's difficulties. Wolfeton House, Charminster, built by an old Dorset family, the Trenchards, in the early sixteenth century shows this well. The original house, with its gatehouse, towers and courtyard, was still based on the medieval plan of a great hall with cross-wings. By the late sixteenth century, however, this was considered inconvenient and unsuitable and a massive extension was constructed to provide sitting rooms and a fashionable long gallery, all given a symmetrical elevation. Two other houses which show the same problem are Up Cerne Manor House and Mapperton House. At Up Cerne the medieval hall and cross-wings were left intact but a new arrangement of rooms was added behind them in the early sixteenth century. But the attempt to fit a symmetrical front with a central doorway and three gables at the same time led to an extremely inconvenient rearrangement of rooms and a somewhat unsuccessful front elevation.[5] At Mapperton, which was rebuilt as late as the mid-seventeenth century, the by then archaic hall and cross-wings were kept and a symmetrical front elevation achieved, but only at the expense of a large, untidy and rambling block of other rooms at the rear.

Even the most advanced houses of one period were often radically altered to meet the fashions of another. Iwerne Steepleton House was built early in the seventeenth century on an almost identical plan to Hanford House near by. But in the mid-eighteenth century its central court-yard was roofed over and large flanking pavilions were added. By the 1660s Classical design reigned supreme. There are countless examples of this type of house showing great variation in the standards of design. Thus at Fontmell House, at Iwerne Courtney, the original façade is a pleasing example of Restoration architecture of about 1665 remark-able for its high standard of design, while Bettiscombe Manor House represents a typical country house of the early eighteenth century of which only the front is meant to be seen. On a larger scale, Moreton House, built 1742–4, is also of interest for its main elevation has a curious dis-proportionate scale and though undocumented suggests the employment of a local architect largely unversed in the current fashion. At the top end of the scale there is East-bury House, Tarrant Gunville, designed by the great Vanbrugh between 1718 and 1738 for the famous eccentric George (Bubb) Doddington. Though only a fragment now remains of the once magnificent house, it is enough to appreciate the heavy but impressive masterpiece to which

[5] The dating of this house by the Royal Commission is clearly wrong and it is certainly much older than they suggest.

Doddington invited the poets, writers and politicians of his time and entertained them on a lavish scale.

None of these houses, of course, stood in isolation. They were surrounded by gardens and these too changed in layout and design during this period. Evidence is unfortunately usually lacking for almost all the contemporary gardens have been swept away by later alterations. Nevertheless, something of this aspect of the landscape can still be seen and help us to appreciate the original settings of the houses. Of the small, walled, late-medieval gardens nothing remains, though the tiny enclosed areas in front of some of the unaltered sixteenth-century houses, such as Puncknowle Manor House, reflect the private inward-looking nature of the contemporary garden. Similarly, little remains of the often elaborate formal gardens based on Italian and French ideas fashionable in the seventeenth century. The best, though sadly mutilated, is at Cranborne House, rebuilt by the Cecils at the beginning of the seventeenth century. The house itself is a remarkable expression of the architectural interests of an influential servant of the crown in the mixing of Italian and Flemish features with those of a much older and traditional design. The contemporary walled garden made up of nine rectangular units, its 'mount' and terraces can still be traced, though with some difficulty. Other gardens that remain are largely modern reconstructions, such as at Anderson Manor House with its 'knots' of box and yew, and at Athelhampton where the garden is divided by stone walls into compartments all united and composed into a coherent plan. Even so they do illustrate clearly the seventeenth-century ideal of a formal enclosed garden.

There is little to be seen of the larger formal gardens of the later seventeenth century. The best must have been at Kingston Lacey contemporary with the Restoration house there. But this like all the others has been swept away by eighteenth- and nineteenth-century emparking. Occasionally the topographical historian can, with effort, find some traces. At Bryanston, near Blandford Forum, close to the site of the seventeenth-century house long destroyed, are a few low banks and shallow ditches in the meadows of the river Stour. These are the last remnants of an elaborate formal garden dating from the late seventeenth century and now only to be seen complete in one of William Kipp's engravings (Plate 23). The early eighteenth century saw the end of formal gardens and a change to landscape gardening. Rarely do we see a garden of this period, but Dorset has the remains of at least two on very different scales. The largest and most important is at Eastbury House. The house and its gardens were abandoned by the end of the eighteenth century and it is to this that we owe the partial preservation of a remarkable early eighteenth-century garden. The gardens, designed and laid out by Bridgeman, were perhaps the most important work he ever did. They show to perfection the combination of the older tradition of formal garden combined with the newer romantic idea of vistas across parkland, so that the park became the background for the garden.

Originally there was an extremely formal layout around the house, with small walled gardens, terraces, rectangular flower beds, groves and lawns together with a long pool, giving views across a small valley to a set of terraces surmounted by a 'temple'. All this was surrounded by Bridgeman's invention of the ha-ha, a sunken wall or fence to keep animals out and yet invisible from the house. Beyond lay open parkland with plantations of trees arranged into rectangular and triangular copses partially enclosing large areas of grass. Much of this has gone, but the terraces, ha-ha and walled gardens remain, together with two spectacular octagonal mounds, twenty feet high and 40 feet across. These were originally topped by trees and their effect was projected outwards across the park by a series of fourteen smaller mounds arranged in two parallel rows. Most of these still remain too, looking for all the world like rows of Bronze Age burial mounds. The diligent searcher can even find the minute banks which edged the flower-beds, now covered in undergrowth and the six-inch-high copse banks in the park marking the edges of the former plantations.

The other contemporary garden on a much smaller scale is that at West Woodyates Manor near Pentridge. Here a ha-ha still shows the limits of a small five-acre garden with a large prospect mound in one corner of it, all dating from the early eighteenth century when the house itself was refronted.

The wealth accumulated by the great landowners of Dorset at this period was not only restricted to beautifying their houses and gardens. Many, like their predecessors, spent large sums in glorifying their churches. For example, the nave, north aisle and south chapel of Iwerne Courtney church were rebuilt in 1610 by Sir Thomas Freke. The Frekes, originally small farmers, came to Iwerne in the late fifteenth century and soon rose to prominence. Robert Freke, who died in 1592, was Auditor and Teller of the Exchequer during the reigns of Henry VIII and Elizabeth. He became a person of considerable note in the county and greatly enlarged his estates. When he died it was said that he was worth more than £100,000, possibly a million today. His son Sir Thomas, born in 1563, became an M.P. for Dorset and continued to enlarge the family estates not least by marriage to the heiress of a rich London merchant and Alderman of the City who had himself bought a country estate at Burton Bradstock. It was this background which enabled Sir Thomas to pay for the extremely fine work at Iwerne Courtney church.

At a later date the tower of Frampton church was

rebuilt at the expense of one Robert Browne, a descendant of a remarkable local family who were minor tenants of the manor of Frampton until the late fifteenth century. The family moved into commerce in the early sixteenth century and from their resulting wealth bought, not only the manor of Frampton, but that of Bettiscombe and land in Broadwey and elsewhere. The family continued to prosper and the Robert Browne who built the tower at Frampton also rebuilt the family seats at Frampton and Forston near Charminster.

This examination of the upper classes must not allow us to ignore the rest of the populace of Dorset during this period. Their houses are much more numerous if less impressive dwellings. Though there is virtually no documentary evidence, the large numbers of this type of house in the county give it much of its charm. Yet though one's attention is drawn to many of these buildings by virtue of their often delightful appearance—the stone rubble farms, lying deep in the vale of Marshwood (Plate 25), or the whitewashed cob, thatched houses of the chalk valleys—it is the detail of their lay-out which is of most significance. The building materials for example are of infinite variety in Dorset. Ashlar, stone rubble, chalk cob, flint, timber and brick are all used, often in clearly defined geographical areas based on the availability of such materials. But in spite of the variety of building materials one finds a series of fairly standard plans or room arrangements which may be recognised and which are virtually ubiquitous within the county and indeed beyond it. For example, in certain parts of the county, and especially in the south and west, the most common type of larger sixteenth- and seventeenth-century farmhouse has still a basically medieval plan. Such farms usually consist of a large range of three ground-floor rooms with a through passage dividing two of them and with a fireplace originally only in the central room. This central room was the living room or hall, beyond was the parlour, while across the passage was the kitchen and storeroom. Even when much altered, this basic arrangement is still clearly visible from the outside and such buildings can be seen all over the county. Amongst many are Shedbush Farm in Stanton St Gabriel dating from around 1700 and Higher Combe Farm, Rampisham, of the late seventeenth century, both built of stone rubble with thatched roofs while an identical house in Shillingstone dating from the sixteenth century is timber-framed and thatched.

Similarly, one of the commonest types of smaller house of this period is that with only two ground-floor rooms of unequal size, originally the hall and kitchen, the larger having the only fireplace. The type occurs widely in the county regardless of building materials. An improved version, also of two rooms, both with external end chimneys, is the commonest form of small dwelling by the early eighteenth century. At the same time the changes in room arrangement and internal design introduced by the great landowners were reaching the middle levels of society. From now on, most of the new or rebuilt larger farms were planned with the more advanced double-depth arrangement of rooms and usually with some attempt at Classical, or at least symmetrical front elevations.

By double-depth we mean the arrangement of rooms in a house in a way now considered to be normal. That is a house two rooms deep. This idea of room arrangement appeared in Dorset in the seventeenth century, and gradually filtered down the social structure. Before this, all buildings were merely ranges of single room width. Size was increased by extending the range or by turning a corner and making wings. Thus the gradual adoption of the double-depth plan in house design is of outstanding importance to the historian of the landscape as well as to the student of architectural and social history.

In Dorset we can see this slow percolation down the social scale very well indeed. Up to the late seventeenth century only the great houses were of double-depth plan. By the 1750s the process had reached the country gentry and larger farmers. By 1900 almost all new and rebuilt farmhouses and cottages were of this type, and of course today the plan is standard.

One minor aspect of the landscape during the early part of this period was brought about by advances in military techniques. During the 1540s the international, political and military situation resulted in the construction of new defence works to protect the two major harbours of the county. At Weymouth, two castles, Sandsfoot and Portland, were built and at the same time Poole Harbour was defended by a castle on Brownsea Island to cover its narrow entrance. Today all that remains of that on Brownsea is buried in the cellars of the modern house on the site. Sandsfoot is a ruin but Portland Castle still stands largely unaltered. 'Castle' is in fact quite a misleading description of these works which strictly speaking are semicircular gun platforms set around and backed by a large magazine block. Fully equipped they could successfully repulse any enemy attempt to approach the harbours by their substantial fire power.

SELECT BIBLIOGRAPHY

Atkinson, E. H. T. 'Some Abbotsbury Records', *Dorset Procs.*, Vol. 48 (1927).
Bettey, J. H. 'Sir John Tregonwell of Milton Abbey', *Dorset Procs.*, Vol. 90 (1969).
Drew, C. D. 'The Division of the Commons of West Parley', *Dorset Procs.*, Vol. 50 (1928).
Ferris, J. P. 'The Gentry of Dorset on the Eve of the Civil War', *Genealogist Mag.*, Vol. 15, No. 3 (1965).

Fussell, G. E. 'Four Centuries of Farming Systems in Dorset', *Dorset Procs.*, Vol. 73 (1952).
Hutchins, J. *History of Dorset,* 3rd ed., Vols. 1–4 (1864).
Oswald, A. *Country Houses of Dorset* (1959).
R.C.H.M. *Dorset.*
Taylor, C. C. 'Medieval and Later Fields and Field Shapes', *Dorset Procs.*, Vol. 90 (1969).
Warren, P. J. K. 'The Story of Holt Forest', *Dorset Procs.*, Vol. 88 (1967).
Whitehead, B. J. 'Management and Land-Use of Water Meadows in the Frome Valley', *Dorset Procs.*, Vol. 89 (1968).

6. The establishment of the modern landscape, 1750–1900

New settlements and farming. Buildings in the landscape

New settlements and farming

UNTIL THE LATE nineteenth century this period was, on the whole, a prosperous one for Dorset farmers. New agricultural techniques were introduced and became widespread and, especially under the impact of the war economy between 1793 and 1815, there was continuous incentive to specialise and expand agriculture. But whereas in many parts of England this period saw immense changes in the rural landscape, usually as a result of large-scale Parliamentary enclosure of the former common-fields, this type of planned enclosure played only a minor role in Dorset.

Of the nearly 120 Parliamentary Acts of enclosure for the county only half were for the enclosure of common-field arable. And of these half again were only tidying up the last remnants of former common-fields already largely enclosed. So for the 260-odd parishes in the county fewer than thirty actually had large areas of common-fields enclosed by Act of Parliament. Almost everywhere else the common-fields had never existed, or had been enclosed centuries before, or were already largely enclosed as the result of slow private and piecemeal enclosure.

These bare statistics are the measure of the effect of Parliamentary enclosure of the common-fields on the landscape. Some detailed examples will show this much better. When the common-fields of Chesilborne, for example, were enclosed by Act in 1845 less than fifteen per cent of the area of the parish was involved, while at near-by Dewlish where the remaining common-fields were enclosed by Act in 1819 an even smaller proportion was involved. In these and many other parishes where little common-field arable remained, the effect on the landscape of such Acts was negligible. In the few parishes which still had large areas of common-field arable right up to the nineteenth century, the effect of parliamentary enclosure was the more usual complete alteration of the landscape as over so much of the Midlands. All three common-field systems within Piddle-trenthide were removed by Act of Parliament in 1817 and both Pimperne and Winterborne Kingston were both totally enclosed in 1814 and 1848 respectively. Common-fields were also enclosed privately, often by the few remaining landowners. Thus all the common-fields of Burleston disappeared soon after 1848 without any Act of Parliament.

But the large-scale enclosure of common-fields was on the whole rare in the county. It is interesting to note that William Barnes, the one truly rural poet that Dorset has produced and who lived through the later part of this period, never mentioned enclosures of common-fields. He was, however, often concerned with a far more important change in the landscape, the massive break-up of both down-land and heath which took place in these years.

> Oh! no, Poll, no! Since they've a-took
> The common in, our Lew wold nook
> Don't seem a-bit as used to look
> When we had runnen room;
> Girt banks do shut up ev'ry drong,
> An' stratch wi' thorny backs along
> Where we did use to run among
> The vuzzen an' the broom.

Perhaps the main reason for this extensive enclosure of downland and waste was the continued growth of sheep farming, which was carried on in association with complex systems of crop rotation involving four or five courses. This type of agriculture had two effects on the landscape. First, huge areas of water-meadows were laid out to enable more sheep to be kept. By the mid-nineteenth century all the major valleys and many of the smaller ones in the south and centre of the county were interlaced with the water carriages of these meadows, and every river blocked by countless weirs to divert the water into them. It was estimated that there were 6000 acres of water-meadows in the county by the 1830s. Today most are abandoned, and yet in their prime they were as Hardy described them in *The Return of the Native* "meadows watered on a plan so rectangular that on a fine day they look like silver gridirons." The second effect on the landscape, and even more important, was that this form of agriculture demanded enclosed fields for both pasture and new arable, not only in the older arable areas but on the high downlands and heaths. The result of this was the enclosure of both open downland and heathland wastes during this period, on a much larger scale than that which had taken place in the seventeenth century.

These years certainly saw the virtual end of the rolling green Dorset downlands. Some of this enclosure too was affected by Acts of Parliament. In some thirty parishes where common-field arable was enclosed by Act, often on a small scale, huge areas of downland were also included. The downland as well as the common-field arable at Pimperne and Winterborne Kingston, noted above, was enclosed by the same Acts. On the other hand, in at least ten parishes where no common-fields remained Acts of Parliament resulted in the enclosure of all the open downland. Compton Abbas, whose common-fields had long since been enclosed, lost all its downland by Act in 1853. But other large tracts of downland were enclosed without any parliamentary approval. In the 1820s Lord Portman of Bryanston reclaimed all the rough downland of Durweston Common and

Plate 26 The large block of land in the centre of the photograph is Oakley Down, in Wimborne St Giles parish. This chalk downland was enclosed privately during the early part of the nineteenth century, but the geometric lay-out of the fields is typical of the late enclosure of this kind of land whether by Act of Parliament or by private landowners.

Plate 27 The landscape of parliamentary enclosure, at Holwell in the vale of Blackmoor. The road, made up three exactly straight alignments and a wide verge, was laid out by the enclosure commissioners in 1797. On the left of it are contemporary fields whose lay-out marked the end of the forest and waste in the parish. To the right are much older fields, probably dating from the fifteenth or sixteenth centuries when the common-fields were enclosed. The farms and cottages along the road all date from the nineteenth century.

Plate 28 Sherborne Castle in the late eighteenth century. The period ideal of a romantic parkland round a country house. Laid out by Capability Brown, it still remains today largely unspoilt.

Plate 29 Milton Abbas village. The 'old world' appearance of this, the best known of Dorset villages, belies its origin as a model settlement of the late eighteenth century, built to house the inhabitants of the town of Milton Abbas which was swept away to make a park.

Plate 30 More Crichel House and park. Until the mid-eighteenth century the old manor house, on the site of the present one, stood in the village street opposite the church. Then the house was rebuilt and the whole village removed and replaced by the park and lake.

then worked a four-course arable and sheep rotation on it. Even tenant farmers did the same. In the 1830s James Harding of Waterston, near Puddletown, who was farming on only a yearly tenancy, broke up 140 acres of virgin downland and put it down to arable. In 1866 one of the first steam ploughing-engines in the county was used to break up the downland at Alton Pancras. These examples are merely a fraction of what was being done at this time, of which we have almost no record. No exact estimate of the amount of downland broken up can now be made, but it was put at thousands of acres by two independent observers in 1854 and 1872 (Plate 26).

All this enclosure, whether parliamentary or private, on large or small scale, of common-field arable or open downland, produced an entirely new landscape, characterised as elsewhere by large geometrically-shaped fields, usually bounded by quickset hedges on low field banks. However, one feature which so often followed this type of enclosure in other counties, that of new isolated farmsteads in the new fields, was a rarity in the chalklands of Dorset. On the whole, the newly enclosed land continued to be worked from the old village centres. This is not to say that these new enclosures were devoid of buildings. Within a few years of their establishment the fields became dotted with groups of barns and sheds arranged around yards which acted as centres of farming activity. These structures, though now often derelict and disused are still a characteristic feature of the chalk landscape resulting from enclosure.

The heathland areas too underwent large-scale enclosure during this period. Here again enclosure of common-field arable was rare, for little remained, but large areas of open heathland were enclosed and put under the plough. Some of this was done by Act of Parliament as one would expect. About a dozen parishes in the south and east of the county lost almost all of their open heathland in this way during the nineteenth century. The heathland of Combe Keynes disappeared entirely in 1761, that of Hampreston in 1813 and of East Stoke in 1870, all as a result of parliamentary action. In addition large landowners also brought great tracts of heathland under cultivation without such acts. In the late eighteenth century, Humphrey Sturt of Crichel, whom we shall meet again, was a well-known improving landlord. Part of his large estate included Brownsea Island in Poole Harbour, and here he reclaimed some 900 acres of land by burning off the heath and planting it with clover and trees. Though today it has reverted to heath, the low banks bounding the former fields and copses can still be seen on winter days when the bracken has died down. At the same time William Frampton of Moreton was one of many who enclosed large parts of their heathland estates. Once again these newly enclosed lands are characterised today by geometrically-shaped fields, largely devoid of farmsteads. In addition, a great amount of small-scale and piecemeal enclosure took place.

This gave rise to tiny, often irregularly as well as geometrically shaped fields, usually associated with isolated farmsteads, cottages and hamlets. Much of this enclosure was carried out by small farmers or by 'squatters'. This latter form of enclosure occurred widely in the nineteenth century and provided the land to accommodate the rapidly rising rural population. Enclosure by squatters appears to have been the origin of a plot of five acres of land in Lychett Minster parish which when sold in 1788 was described as being "taken from the common". On the other hand, enterprising small farmers also reclaimed much land. One of William Frampton's tenants at Moreton was a William White who "by severe self denial and the most exhausting industry" raised himself from the status of a day labourer to that of a farmer with 120 acres, sixteen of which he enclosed from the heath by his own hand.

The results of this kind of enclosure may be seen all over the Dorset heathlands. At Moreton itself there is a group of cottages on the heathland with small closes around it, known as New Moreton in the early nineteenth century, which is of late-eighteenth or early-nineteenth-century date. Similarly in Steeple parish, until the late eighteenth century, the only settlements and fields north of the Purbeck Ridge were those of West Creech and Creech Grange, both in existence by 1086 and both on the heathland edge. But during the late eighteenth and nineteenth centuries a whole series of cottages and smallholdings with names such as Broadmoor, Steeple Leaze and Rookery Cottages, each with a few small irregularly-shaped fields, appeared all over the heathland (Plate 12).

In the wooded claylands the same process of enclosure occurred, here continuing the centuries-old clearance of the forests and wastes. Again it produced the familiar geometrically-shaped fields, but also isolated farmsteads and cottages. This was partly no doubt because of the tradition of building such farms here, and partly because of the large-scale movement of squatters on to the new wide road verges and the consequent erection of cottages there.

The major large enclosures were again carried out both by Act of Parliament and by private agreement. Nearly twenty Acts were passed to carry through enclosure of woodland and waste in the Blackmoor Vale alone. By an Act of 1797 almost a third of the parish of Holwell, where medieval and later enclosure had not been on a large scale, was divided up into regular-shaped fields (Plate 27). At Buckland Newton, where earlier enclosure had been common, only three small and widely separated pieces of waste remained to be enclosed by an Act of 1854. At Marnhull some 300 acres of land in the south-east corner of the parish appear to have been enclosed privately in the late eighteenth century, to judge by the field-shapes and the dates of the two isolated farmhouses there. Likewise at Glanvilles Wootton 200 acres of land in the east of the parish, which is shown as open common on the Tithe Map of 1839, was subsequently divided into extremely long rectangular fields. In them are two farmsteads, both dated 1847. In the clay-lands too there was much piecemeal enclosure at this time. One example is the '16 luggs' of land described in a docu-ment of 1812 as being "in a late common", in Cann parish. This particular piece of land is in an area of small fields, on heavy clay land near the edge of an existing piece of common. It must represent the latest stage in a long process of small-scale enclosure.

Despite the massive attack on the commons and wastes during the nineteenth century, Dorset, like many other counties, retains a considerable area of untouched common land. There are no completely accurate figures, but the most reliable recent account shows that there are still some fifty-nine commons covering 8118 acres. If we add the 'fuel allotments' created by the enclosure awards, the total is some 8487 acres. Two-thirds of this acreage lies, as we might expect, on the ancient heathlands, the largest by far being the continuous stretch of Arne, Middlebere, Slepe, and Stoborough Heath—a huge stretch of 1906 acres to the south-east of Wareham.[1]

The prosperity and expansion of agriculture in the county was ended sharply in the late nineteenth century by the general agricultural depression. The county lost 100,000 sheep at this time and large parts of the recently broken up and enclosed land were abandoned. In one parish alone, Sydling St Nicholas, some 800 acres of downland was

[1] For a list of the known commons and their acreages see W. G. Hoskins and L. Dudley Stamp, *The Common Lands of England and Wales* (1963), pp. 267–70. See also the *Report of the Royal Commission on Common Lands* (1958), pp. 209–11, where the figures given differ somewhat from those in Hoskins and Stamp. The figures given by the latter are probably more reliable as they were revised by the late Sir Dudley Stamp after the Commission's Report.

put down to grass again. In many places today on the higher parts of the chalk and limestone hills of the county, we can still see the characteristic low three yards wide ridge-and-furrow or 'narrow rig' of the late-eighteenth- and nineteenth-century ploughing, which remains as an indication of the great expansion of arable land and as a memorial to its decline. On the heathlands too, low earthen banks of former fields often appear after summer fires to indicate where the nineteenth-century farmers once enclosed and ploughed.

Buildings in the landscape

As with the earlier periods this time saw the expansion and prosperity of the county reflected in its contemporary buildings. For the great landlords much wealth continued to come from their Dorset estates, but as time went on, new people with other and very different sources of income came into the county to enhance and enlarge many of the existing country houses and erect new ones.

Many of the older houses were rebuilt or enlarged out of all recognition as their owners kept abreast of new designs, fashions and aspirations. Some of the long established families did this more than once. The original house at Melbury Sampford was gradually altered by the Strangways family. It was refronted in the late seventeenth century and finally greatly enlarged in the late eighteenth century in a restrained and not unpleasing Neo-Gothic style. Other houses were altered both by old families and by new blood and wealth coming in. At Parnham House near Beaminster, the original fifteenth-century house of medieval plan, built by the Strode family, was rebuilt by them in the sixteenth century and enlarged in the early seventeenth century by the addition of a large kitchen block. The family again altered, enlarged and refronted the house in the middle of the eighteenth century to keep up with the latest fashions. Then in 1764 the house passed to the Oglanders, a wealthy Isle of Wight family, and in 1810 they made further additions to designs by John Nash. Today we see it apparently as a mainly early-nineteenth-century composition in the Romantic Gothic style. But closer inspection reveals the continuous story of its development from the medieval house of a small Dorset squire to the large country house of a wealthy nineteenth-century family.

The effect of new families with new wealth rising into the aristocracy after 1750 is also clearly visible in the landscape. One of the most interesting examples is Came House, southeast of Dorchester, perhaps the best Palladian country house in the county. It was built in 1756 by John Damer, the younger brother of Joseph Damer who bought Milton Abbey House at this time and who rose meteorically to become Earl of Dorchester. Came House lies in a magnificent park, deep in the South Winterborne valley, carefully positioned on slightly rising ground. Its superb north front, with imposing portico and a pediment containing the Damer arms, epitomises gracious eighteenth-century design and living.

A near-contemporary building with very different origins is Merley House, south of Wimborne Minster, overlooking the river Stour. It is the product of an eighteenth-century connoisseur Ralph Willet, who claimed to have designed it himself. He was the son of a wealthy West Indies sugar planter, whose accumulated colonial wealth was lavished on the house and estate. The house, erected between 1756 and 1760, is a typical example of its period with the usual pediment and balustrades. It is of particular interest, in view of the source of Willet's wealth, to note that the library ceiling there, which was ornamented with reliefs intended to trace "the rise and progress of civilisation", was supported in its four corners by sugar-cane motifs.

The changes in sources of wealth as well as architectural design by the nineteenth century can be well seen at Canford Manor near Poole. Here an older house was greatly enlarged in 1848 by Sir Charles Barry to include a great hall, gallery and tower. "In its pronounced medievalism and asymmetrical grouping it is a characteristic product of the Gothic Revival."[2] The work was done for a new owner, Sir John Guest, a typical product of the Industrial Revolution. The Guests were originally a small Shropshire family, one of whose members emigrated to South Wales in 1747 and settled in Dowlais, where they became successful iron masters. Sir John, the grandson of the original iron master, became M.P. for Merthyr Tydfil and was created a Baronet in 1838. To continue the rapid rise into the aristocracy, which his son, later created Lord Wimborne, completed, Sir John bought Canford in the 1840s and quickly enlarged it.

One of the largest and one of the last of the long line of country houses was erected by Lord Portman in the 1890s at Bryanston near Blandford Forum (Plate 24). It is a superb example of late Victorian aristocratic attitudes. The earlier medieval and eighteenth-century house at Bryanston lay down on the edge of the river Stour. The new one was set uncompromisingly on a virgin site high on the downs, dominating the landscape and overlooking the estates of its owner, both rural and urban. The design too reflects the same attitude. By Norman Shaw, in his 'Queen Anne' style, it is somewhat clumsy in detail and twice as elaborate as any real eighteenth-century house. It may not be a building of great beauty, but it sums up completely the effect on the landscape of late Victorian grandeur. It is now a public school.

The gardens and parks of these houses also reflect the changing fashions and ideas of the four or five generations between 1750 and 1900. By the 1750s all the older formal gardens were being swept away and replaced by large

[2] A. Oswald, *The Country Houses of Dorset* (1935).

159

landscaped parks, which were to dominate and beautify much of the Dorset landscape up to the present day. The gracious parks, grassy slopes, lakes and carefully positioned woods, copses and isolated trees at places such as Sherborne Castle (Plate 28), Wimborne St Giles House, and Melbury Sampford House are all the legacy of late eighteenth-century landscape gardeners who often altered the land around these houses beyond recognition. The best known of all is of course Milton Abbas. There Joseph Damer, Viscount Milton and later Earl of Dorchester, rebuilt the house between 1771 and 1776 in a severe Classical style, and went on to create a park around it which involved the complete removal of the adjacent little town of Milton Abbas. This "unmannerly imperious lord" as Sir William Chambers, the designer of the house, called Damer, ordered the town to be swept away and the whole area landscaped by 'Capability' Brown. The removal of the inhabitants to a new model village (Plate 29) half a mile away was not in fact achieved without a struggle, and it took nearly twenty years (1771–90) before Damer achieved his plan. Whatever we may think of his methods, there can be no doubt that the park as we see it today, in full maturity, set in the steep-sided valley, surrounded by trees and with its lake directing the eye towards the exquisite grouping of House and Abbey Church is one of the great glories of Dorset.

Less well known but of equal interest is the story of Crichel House and its park. The old manor house lay in the village of More Crichel in the bottom of the wide valley of the Crichel brook. In 1742 when the existing seventeenth century house was burnt down it was surrounded by a small enclosed formal garden. The Napier family who owned it started to rebuild, but in 1765 the male line failed and the estate passed to a nephew, Humphrey Sturt, of nearby Horton House. Already a wealthy man, he further increased his fortunes by marriage to an heiress. On moving to

Crichel he at once embarked on great alterations and extensions which doubled the size of the house then in process of being built, and made it the magnificent structure we see today. But Sturt was also determined to improve the setting of his new house, and to this end he removed the entire village of More Crichel except for the church, and landscaped the whole area into a carefully contrived parkland with woods, copses and a large serpentine lake (Plate 30). The displaced inhabitants were rehoused in an entirely new village, still called Newtown, a mile away to the south, in Witchampton parish. Unfortunately, only one original house remains of this 'new village'.

Sturt's work at Crichel was not the first attempt at large-scale landscaping carried out by his family. His father, another Humphrey Sturt, had some years earlier undertaken an extensive emparking scheme at Horton House, the family seat, which included not only the construction of Horton Tower, a mighty brick viewing-point, but two large lakes containing over 100 acres of water stretching eastwards from the edge of the house for more than a mile. House and park were all abandoned with the move to Crichel, and only the ruined tower on a hilltop and the great earthen dams of the lakes, buried in the encroaching woodland, remain of this short-lived enterprise.

The formation of large parks continued into the nineteenth century on an increasing scale. Charborough House near Wimborne Minster, originally built in the mid-seventeenth century, was surrounded by formal gardens until the late eighteenth century. From then on work on 'improving' the house and landscaping and emparking the surrounding fields went on for nearly sixty years. A tall romantic tower looking out over the new park was erected in 1790, and the house was altered and enlarged in 1810 and again in 1838. The park was increased in size to the present 800 acres and today, still carrying deer, adds much to the beauty of this part of Dorset. Emparking went on to the end of the century. In 1876 the small house and park at Iwerne Minster were bought by Lord Wolverton, a successful politician and son of a highly successful banker. A vast new baronial mansion was erected (1878–80) and to accompany it, a park of 150 acres, with an ornamental lake, was established in the former arable land.

In the nineteenth century, however, the landscaped park extending right up to the walls of the great house became unfashionable. Instead, a small formalised garden round the house, using the existing park as a backcloth, was favoured. As early as 1835 when Sir Charles Barry was altering Kingston Lacey House, the existing formal terraces and gardens around it were constructed out of the eighteenth-century parkland which had earlier replaced the original late-seventeenth-century formal gardens there. At Crichel, soon after 1900, the house was separated from its parkland by a small formal garden with a little domed 'temple', all of which still exist.

Smaller domestic buildings, as might be expected, exhibit less variety of development. The larger farmhouses and dwellings of the lesser gentry were almost always built of brick, all with symmetrical elevations and double-depth plans. They were usually slightly behind the fashions of the time, so that typically late-eighteenth-century designs appear in the early nineteenth century, and Regency styles continued until well after 1850. The smaller houses of the labouring classes, while often retaining certain regional characteristics imposed by building materials, were built increasingly to a common plan consisting of two adjacent rooms with a chimney on each gable end. The majority of the nineteenth-century squatters' cottages on the roadside verges and on encroachments in the heathlands are of this type.

Like all other parts of the country, Dorset acquired for

better or worse a fine array of new, rebuilt and 'restored' churches during this period. Few are of any architectural merit. Three examples will show the variety of styles and more important some of the varied reasons for their construction. The church at the new village of Milton Abbas erected by Joseph Damer in 1786 for the displaced inhabitants of the old town, is an interesting example of the late eighteenth-century Gothic revival. Another in similar style is that at Fleet, near Weymouth, built 1827–9 at the expense of George Gould. He was the last of a line of a family of Devon gentry who migrated to Dorset in the sixteenth century and who became wealthy merchants. Unmarried and rector of Fleet, he was left all the family's estates in 1818 when his elder brother, also unmarried, died. With no one to whom to bequeath the family fortunes, he rebuilt his church at his own expense when the old one was destroyed in a storm. The church at Oborne, in the north of the county, erected in 1861–2 in a simple Early English style, was paid for by very different methods. Its site and £500 were given by Gonville and Caius College, Cambridge, the lords of the manor, and another £450 by the other major landowner in the parish. Fifty pounds was added by two Church building societies, £110 was collected by the parish and the remainder made up by subscription.

The last of the great defensive works of the county is the massive Citadel or fort, built at the Verne, on the highest point of the Isle of Portland in the 1860s. Together with the breakwaters it was designed to protect Weymouth Harbour following the invasion scare of 1859. Though now sadly mutilated and difficult of access, the towering structure with its gunports, emplacements and magazines still dominates the whole area, and remains as much a monument to nineteenth-century ideas of warfare as the better-known Maiden Castle does to the Iron Age or Corfe Castle to the medieval period.

SELECT BIBLIOGRAPHY

Fussell, G. E. 'Four Centuries of Farming Systems in Dorset', *Dorset Procs.*, Vol. 73 (1952).
Oswald, A. *Country Houses of Dorset* (1959).
R.C.H.M. *Dorset*.

7. Industry, road and rail

UNLIKE MANY COUNTIES Dorset has been little affected by
industry at any period of its history. This is not to say that
there are no industrial landscapes in the county but that they
are fairly localised and not always destructive in landscape
terms. The industries of Dorset fall into two clearly defined
types, the extractive industries and a variety of what may
generally be called textile industries.

The oldest of the extractive industries is that of stone
quarrying. Much of this was on a very limited scale in most
parts of the county and is now visible only in the form of
small overgrown and long abandoned quarries from which
limestone and greensand were taken to build the churches or
great houses, or chalk to provide clunch and cob for the
cottages. But in the south and south-east of the county the
stone industry based on the underlying Jurassic limestone
rocks was, and still is, on a much greater scale. On and
around the Isle of Portland, the Portland beds produce a
building stone of the highest quality while in Purbeck, as
well as building stone, the famous Purbeck 'marble' is
found. These two areas were already producing stone in the
Roman period and were greatly exploited during medieval
times.

Portland stone was being used extensively for local
buildings by the twelfth century—Rufus Castle, Portland, is
constructed from it. But it was in the thirteenth and fourteenth centuries that the industry at Portland became more
than locally important. By the early fourteenth century
stone was being shipped from the island to a variety of
places. It was certainly being used at Exeter Cathedral at
this time and a considerable amount was also used at
Westminster Palace and the Tower of London. The most

important development of the Portland stone industry took place in the seventeenth century, when Inigo Jones, after a personal visit, chose it for the Banqueting Hall, Westminster, and the York Gate at Greenwich Hospital. Later Wren adopted Portland stone for St Paul's Cathedral and for all the other London churches he designed after the Fire of London. From then on millions of tons of stone were sent from the island. Until the late nineteenth century when the railway reached Portland most of this stone was shipped out, either by loading the ships at the quarries cut in the cliffs, or from small piers. Some of the latter still exist, often now either derelict or much altered, as at Church Ope Cove on the south-east side of the island. The island itself is deeply scarred by this industry. Large parts of it are covered by vast open quarries, many still in operation (Plate 31) and elsewhere are numerous small abandoned workings.

The Purbeck 'marble' industry had a somewhat earlier flowering. Even by the twelfth century the marble was prized for its decorative qualities and was widely used not only in Dorset but far beyond for small-scale sculptures such as fonts, etc. But in the thirteenth century, new architectural ideas resulted in an enormous development of the industry and its products were exported all over the country and abroad. The cathedrals of Salisbury, Winchester, Worcester, Wells and Exeter, Westminster Abbey and countless small parish churches used it extensively and thousands of tombs, coffin slabs and fonts were made from it. By the middle of the fourteenth century the industry began to decline due to changing architectural fashions as well as the increasing use of other rocks such as alabaster more suitable for detailed carving. Yet the marble continued to be quarried in considerable quantities until the seventeenth century and even later, and the quarrying of building stone was always important.

The remains of this industry may still be seen in Purbeck.

The surface of the limestone plateau of south Purbeck is scarred by hundreds of abandoned and overgrown medieval quarries, with later ones less overgrown, and a few still working. Close to the sea, as at Winspit at Worth Matravers, large quarries cut into the cliff faces where stone was loaded directly into ships, still remain. But the history of quarrying here is reflected in other remains too. Deeply worn hollow-ways and long-abandoned lanes run north and north-west from the quarries towards Corfe Castle, where the masons and sculptors who worked the stone lived, and whither the marble and stone were brought. Beyond the narrow Corfe gap through the Purbeck hills further lanes and hollow-ways can still be traced across the heath towards the south shore of Poole Harbour, marking the routes taken by the shaped stone and carved marble. There, the remains of quays and wharves still exist at the remote hamlets of Redcliffe, Slepe and Ower, the only indications of once bustling loading places where the stone was transferred to ships bound for other parts of Britain and the continent. Ships such as the "Margarete of Wareham of 48 tons burden" which when arrested by the Keepers of the Port of Poole in 1374 was carrying "two high tombs of marble for the Earl of Arundel and his wife" and "one great stone for the Bishop of Winchester."

Another extractive industry close to Purbeck which has left its mark on the landscape is clayworking. The clays around Poole Harbour were used from prehistoric times onwards for local earthenware products, but in the eighteenth century an export trade in raw clay developed when it was discovered that good quality china could be made from it. By the end of the century, some 10,000 tons a year were being shipped from the region and the industry continued to flourish until the late nineteenth century. Abandoned and still working clay pits are still a feature of the south-east Dorset heathland. Amongst the largest of the abandoned pits are those near the south shore of Poole Harbour on Newton Heath which are now slowly disappearing under a cloak of bracken and gorse. But it is still possible to find traces of the mineral lines which joined and ran north on a high embankment along the Goathorn peninsula to a quay at its northern end on the edge of the deep water channel.

Other remains of extractive industries survive in the landscape sometimes to puzzle the unwary. One such instance is at Kimmeridge Bay, on the coast. High above the cliffs and apparently cutting off a small promontory from the land to the north is a curious 'intrenchment' which many older antiquarians and some modern archaeologists have taken to be a promontory fort of the Iron Age. Yet if we examine it carefully we see that it consists of a series of embankments and cuttings, carefully graded on a falling slope. It is in fact a tramway, heading for a still-existing stone pier in the bay. Its precise date is not known, but it is certainly of seventeenth- or eighteenth-century origin and is probably to be connected with the extraction of the Kimmeridge shale, a soft, bituminous mudstone, which was worked at this time for alum and for fuel by various speculators, all of whom consistently failed to make money out of the enterprise.[1]

The varied local textile industries, of which there were many in Dorset from the sixteenth century onwards, such as button and stocking making, and rope and sail manufacture, have left little trace in the landscape. They were all mainly cottage industries whose remains have now disappeared. But others which were to a certain extent mechanised in the eighteenth and nineteenth centuries have left evidence of their former existence. Thus in the extreme north of the county in the village of Bourton is an early nineteenth-century textile mill, now a modern factory, and quite out of

[1] For a recent article on the alum industry, see *Somerset and Dorset Notes and Queries*, Vol. 29 (1969), pp. 81–4.

Plate 31 Stone quarry, Portland. One of the hundreds of workings, large and small, which scar the landscape here. This area is the only part of the county which has been spoilt by industry.

Plate 32   Blandford Forum. The busy market occupies the Market Place which is surrounded by delightful eighteenth-century houses and shops and domi-nated by the splendid town hall and church. All were built within a few years

Plate 33 Burley House, Lyme Regis. Built about 1835 on the outskirts of the town. A typical example of the better-class houses erected towards the end of the town's era as a fashionable resort.

Plate 34 Belvidere Terrace, Melcombe Regis. One of the later seafront terraces in the town. Building started about 1820 and continued sporadically, although to a uniform elevation, until its final completion in 1855. Largely unspoilt, it reflects the early nineteenth-century importance of the town as a fashionable resort.

Plate 35 Wareham from the air. The photograph, taken in 1946, shows how even then the town was largely confined within its Saxon walls. Only in recent years has the familiar suburban sprawl reached out beyond the original defences

place in rural Dorset. It stands on the edge of an artificial pool. The whole complex is the remains of a water-powered linen spinning mill built in 1800 when the old cottage industry was mechanised by an enterprising local manufacturer. Near by, at Gillingham, where a local silk spinning industry grew up in the late eighteenth century, there is an early nineteenth-century building of some interest. The ground and first floors of the long brick structure were designed for washing and drying the spun silk. The upper floor, a single large room with a low ceiling and small dormer windows, was a dormitory for young girl apprentices who were brought down from London workhouses at the ages of ten or eleven to work in the mill.

Two other normally important aspects of the landscape of the Industrial Revolution, canals and railways, affected Dorset little or not at all. Only one canal was ever planned and that was never constructed. The county had no major industrial seaports to attract railways and only a few lines were ever built. Most of these were over relatively easy country and involved few major engineering works. The only difficult line was that from Yeovil to Dorchester, opened in 1857, which climbed over the broken country of west Dorset. This line has many embankments and cuttings as well as four tunnels. But even here only two of the tunnels were constructed because of natural obstacles. The other two were forced upon the Railway Company for very different reasons, one not unusual in railway history, the other probably unique. The 700-yard tunnel at Frampton was cut so that the railway would not spoil the landscaped parkland of Frampton Court through which it was to pass. The one under the Iron Age hill fort of Poundbury, just outside Dorchester, was built following a public outcry at the threatened destruction of the hill fort. Also worth mentioning in this context is the protest against the Railway Company over Maumbury Rings, the Neolithic ritual monument and Roman amphitheatre at Dorchester. When the company proposed a line which would have cut through the Rings, a battle ensued in which the local people won the day. The result is the very tight curve out of Dorchester South station which still slows trains to this day.

Now many of the railways of the county have been abandoned and Dorset is served by only one main line. The familiar picture of empty stations and deserted tracks can be seen in many places. The line across the east Dorset heathland from Salisbury to Wimborne Minster, opened with the usual ceremonies in 1861, lasted only just over 100 years, and parts of it have already disappeared under the heathland vegetation. Such is the transitory nature of some of man's impact on the landscape.

Man's earlier lines of communication, roads, have in many cases survived much better. The county has some remarkable stretches of Roman roads amongst which Ackling Dyke, the road south from the Roman predecessor of Salisbury, is one of the best examples in Britain. South of Bokerley Dyke and close to the modern Dorchester–Salisbury road, it survives as a magnificent raised causeway driving straight across the downs.

The history and development of the medieval roads of Dorset have been surveyed at length elsewhere.[2] Yet much research remains to be done. The deep winding lanes in the claylands of the vale of Blackmoor and in the west of the county which help to make those parts so attractive are still not fully understood. How did they come into existence? They wander from farm to farm in a most inexplicable way, often taking little account of the natural landscape. Are they the remains of prehistoric trackways through the forest, boundaries of Saxon estates (Saxon charters and much later estate maps suggest that some might be) or are they merely convenient links between the farmsteads that grew up in

[2] Good, *The Old Roads of Dorset* (1966).

these areas over the centuries? We do not know. It may be, too, that many of the minor lanes and roads originated as double-ditched boundaries *between* farms, as they did in Devon. A close examination of farm-boundaries as shown on the Tithe maps of the 1840s might well throw light on this possibility.

Most of the broad downland drove-roads which sprawled across the ridgeways in the chalklands have long since disappeared as such and become either narrow lanes or wide main roads. Most of them went in the late eighteenth- and nineteenth-century enclosure of these downlands, but a picture of what they were like is preserved in that priceless document of the English landscape, the first edition of the Ordnance Survey one-inch map, published for Dorset in 1811.

Of the more recent roads, those resulting from parliamentary enclosure are the most impressive though they are common only on the heathland. Here are splendid lengths of straight wide roads which were often the realignment of older tracks. Many of the present main roads in the county are quite late in origin when Turnpike Trusts, local government bodies and local lords carried out road improvements and alterations. The first Dorset Turnpike Act was for a section of the 'Great Western Post Road'—now called the A30—between Shaftesbury and Sherborne in 1752. The last act was that of 1840 setting up the Puddletown and Wimborne Trust, if one excludes a minor act for building a bridge in 1857.[3]

One of the most interesting of these late roads is the present A31 from Wimborne Minster to Puddletown. Today it is a major trunk road and yet until the middle of the nineteenth century it was merely a collection of narrow lanes winding from village to village. In 1841 the Wimborne

[3] For a detailed discussion of the turnpike roads, see Ch. VI of Good, *The Old Roads of Dorset*.

and Puddletown Turnpike Trust was established and about £24,000 was spent in buying land and constructing a virtually new road. It was an unfortunate time, for the railway came, traffic did not materialise and the investors lost money. Its heyday did not come until the twentieth century when the motor-car took over from the short-lived railways.

SELECT BIBLIOGRAPHY

Drury, D. G. 'The Use of Purbeck Marble in Medieval Times', *Dorset Procs.*, Vol. 70 (1948).
Good, R. *The Old Roads of Dorset* (1966).
Lucking, J. H. *Railways of Dorset* (1968).
R.C.H.M. *Dorset.*
Warren, F. C. 'Dorset Industries of the Past', *Dorset Procs.*, Vol. 59 (1937).

8. The landscape of towns

*Market towns. Extended market towns. Ports. Planned
towns. Resort towns. Dorchester*

THERE ARE OVER twenty places in Dorset which either
still are, or were once considered to be urban areas. Today
these vary from the vast suburban sprawl of Poole to the
bare windswept Newton Heath not far away, the site of
an abortive thirteenth-century town. All these places had
various origins and much of their history is still visible in
their present appearance. But in most cases we have to look
beyond the existing buildings and examine in detail the
lay-out of streets and lanes, the shape and size of building
plots, and the form and date of buildings hidden behind
later façades. We must look for long-abandoned banks and
ditches and take note of every street-name. We must journey
into the modern hubbub of a seaside resort in August, and
climb the bare slopes of chalk downland on a winter's day.
Only then can we begin to understand the topography of
the towns of Dorset.

It would be quite impossible here to describe in detail all
the towns of the county. We must limit ourselves to a
consideration of the salient features of some, and con-
centrate on a few places in more detail.

Market towns

All parts of England developed over the centuries a multitude of small market towns, not only in the countryside but
of it. Dorset was no exception, and based on the agricultural

wealth of the county a whole series of little towns grew up here. Most of these always were and still are fairly small and rarely of more than local significance. But they are of interest in terms of their origin and development and, in some cases, decline.

Many of them grew out of existing villages by reason of the early establishment of minster churches or religious houses near by, which thus gave them greater prosperity than adjacent settlements. *Beaminster* and *Sturminster Newton*, though both little more than overgrown villages today, undoubtedly grew to have a local importance because of the early existence of the minster churches there. Each still has a small market place at its centre, marked by a widening of the street but in both instances these have been encroached upon by later buildings. In both towns the modern successors of the great minster churches stand some distance away from these commercial centres, aloof and somewhat remote from the formerly busy streets.

Two places even smaller now are *Cerne Abbas* and *Abbotsbury*. Both were once important by virtue of the adjacent great monastic houses but have long since declined into sleepy villages since the dissolution of the abbeys ended their prosperity. They show their former importance in their present lay-out and again they lie some distance from the monastic sites. At Cerne the main thoroughfare, Long Street, widens considerably in the middle of its length and though again this now has encroachments on it, it is clearly the original market place of the town. Similarly at Abbotsbury the north-west end of the market street widens to form a large triangular open space.

In the extreme north of the county are two other small market towns, or former towns, with very different appearances. In the north-east is *Cranborne,* now a small village miles from any major road. Before the Norman Conquest it too had its own monastic house, which may have given it some status. But far more important is the fact that until the eighteenth century it lay on the main road from Salisbury to the south, lying midway between it and Wimborne Minster. Its rustic cob and timber cottages and rural appearance belie its former importance and stand in sharp contrast to the other town, *Gillingham*, at the north end of the vale of Blackmoor. Here we find a small town almost entirely built of brick whose development deep in a former forested area was late. It was in fact little more than a village throughout the medieval period and really only grew to any size with the modest development of a local textile industry in the eighteenth century. This fact combined with a disastrous fire which destroyed most of it in 1694 accounts for the present character of the town, though the tasteless aristocratic benevolence in the mid-nineteenth century of the Duke of Westminster, whose seat lay near by, has not enhanced its appearance.

MILTON ABBAS If Gillingham is not amongst the most attractive of Dorset market towns at least it is still there. One such town has not reached the present century intact. This is Milton Abbas in the deep wooded chalk valley of the Milborne Brook in central Dorset. In origin it was one of a long line of small villages along the valley, but the existence and growth of the large Benedictine monastery there led understandably to its development as a small town. It certainly grew in size and importance with its own market and fairs and by 1333 there were between 400 and 500 inhabitants, a populous place for Dorset. The dissolution of the abbey in the sixteenth century had little effect on the town, centred as it was in a rich and prosperous agricultural area. Then between 1771 and 1790 the town was completely demolished by Viscount Milton to make way for the new park around his house (*see* p. 160). The new park wall was five and a quarter miles around, a massive feature in the local landscape. The little town came to a dramatic end. Not without all trace, however, for in the park south of the house the old urban lay-out is still preserved by banks, ditches and hollows (Fig. 16).

The medieval market place and High Street are now buried under three feet of earth, but beyond, Broad Street is still visible as a wide hollow-way together with other streets and back lanes and along all of them are the remains of houses and their gardens. The gardens on the hill slope on the east side of the town are especially interesting for there one can still see the grass-grown remains of the individual layouts lying about the house sites. Some have small terraces, others garden paths and most even have traces of what appear to be pig-sties at their extremities.

CORFE CASTLE Corfe must vie with Blandford Forum as the most attractive of Dorset market towns. It lies under the shadow of the great hill in the centre of the Corfe Gap dominated by the stark remains of the massive castle itself (Plate 15). It undoubtedly grew up under the patronage of this castle built by William the Conquerer probably on the site of a Saxon royal palace.[1] The importance of the castle certainly gave rise to the early growth of the town but its greatest period of expansion came with the rapid development of the Purbeck marble industry in the thirteenth century. Corfe had a market as early as 1215 and a fair in 1246, and was taxed as a borough from the early fourteenth century. It grew up along two roads from the south which converged at the foot of the castle to pass through the Corfe Gap. In spite of its medieval importance, there are now few remains of medieval houses there. Most of the present houses in the village date from the sixteenth and early seventeenth centuries and reflect the prosperity of the

[1] Though M. W. Beresford includes Corfe (admittedly speculatively) in his list of Medieval New Towns.

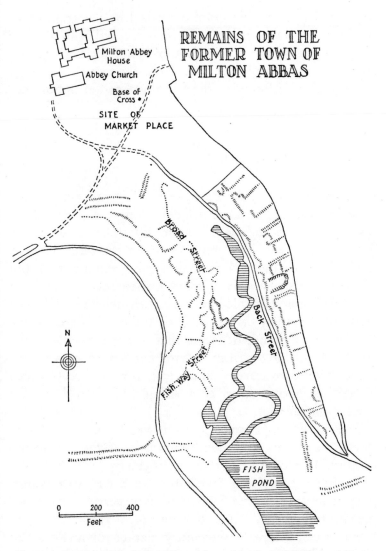

Fig. 16. In the park, below the abbey church and Milton Abbey House, the remains of the greater part of the town of Milton Abbas are preserved. All the main streets are visible as well as most of the sites of the houses. On the hillside above Back Street the varied lay-out of the individual gardens can be easily seen. *Based on a plan by R. C. H. M.* (*Crown Copyright Reserved*).

M

town at this time which is also marked by the granting of full borough status in 1576. These houses, all of local stone with stone slate roofs, are of an exceptionally high quality and indicate not only the wealth but the craftsmanship of their builders. After 1650 the town declined in importance with the ending of the stone industry, and this too is seen in the later buildings in the town. These, though in the same tradition of design and materials, fall far below the earlier ones in their quality.

BLANDFORD FORUM Blandford originated once again as one of a line of small settlements along the north side of the river Stour. Indeed in Domesday Book it cannot be differentiated from five other places in the same area, all with the same name and all small farming communities. But its position at a major river crossing where several important early roads converged led to its early growth and by the late thirteenth century it had acquired the additional name Forum or Chipping, denoting that it was a market town, and distinguishing it from its rural neighbours of the same name. The town developed along two main streets which joined just above the river crossing with a small market place at the junction.

The present appearance of the town, however, is due to disastrous events and their aftermath in the eighteenth century. The town was partly destroyed by fire in 1713 and then almost completely levelled by an even worse conflagration in 1731. In the following sixty years it was completely rebuilt and thus remains as a particularly fine example of an eighteenth-century market town (Plate 32). The architecture of this virtually new town is greatly enhanced by the fact that the work of reconstruction was controlled to a large extent by two local builders, the brothers John and William Bastard, both gifted with an aptitude for design that bordered on genius. The Bastards planned and supervised much of the rebuilding, which followed the old street plan. Their finest work was the parish church, completed in 1739, in the Classical style. The Town Hall, also by the Bastards and dated 1734, stands in the Market Place. It is a most attractive building of Portland stone with a ground floor arcade leading into a stone-flagged loggia known as The Shambles. The whole building is surmounted by an elaborately carved cornice and a pediment. The houses of the town are of more than ordinary interest. Though all basically similar in appearance, both variety and unity were obtained by special brick bonding and by the use of bricks of various colours. For example, dark red brick was used to outline window openings and quoins, and pale red bricks to define window heads, all set in a background of blue bricks. More important is that all the new houses were not only carefully designed for different social classes but also erected in distinct 'zones' for those classes. There are a number of large houses with symmetrical elevations and ornate central doorways for the professional and merchant classes on the outskirts of the town. In the centre of the town, for shopkeepers and lesser merchants, are smaller houses with the entrance to one side, while in between are the working-class houses often built in pairs, sharing a common central entrance door and passage. The town remains a remarkable period piece which has been little altered, for nineteenth-century and later development has taken place on the rising ground to the north-east and scarcely intrudes on the town centre at all. In fact it remains much as it was described over a century ago, "one of the most cheerful and handsome in the county."[2]

Extended market towns

Amongst the smaller market towns of the county, two stand

[2] Murray's *Handbook for Dorset* (1856).

out because both had new parts deliberately grafted on to them in the medieval period. The first of these is *Sherborne*. It was an old town, which grew up at an important route-centre and river crossing, but it was given a great impetus by reason of the existence of a minster church which from the eighth century was also the centre of a huge bishopric. Despite the loss of its ecclesiastical status in the eleventh century it continued to grow under the shadow of its great abbey. But in 1227–8 the Bishop of Salisbury, having just established his new town of New Salisbury, founded a new borough called Sherborne Newlands immediately outside the old town. It consisted merely of a single street, still called Newland, between the town and the Bishop's castle and little remains today, except the name, to indicate its origins.

WIMBORNE MINSTER   Here the evidence for an additional borough grafted on to an older town is much clearer in the landscape (Fig. 17). The town lies on the north bank of the river Stour at the point where the tiny river Allen joins it. Today it is still a small town, with a mass of narrow winding streets which are a planner's nightmare, completely dominated by the great minster church, a superb specimen of twelfth-century architecture. Again the town's development must lie with the establishment of this minster church, though the remains of a Roman building, still visible under the church, probably reflects a much earlier beginning. By 1086 the town was of some importance for a number of burgesses are recorded there in Domesday Book. Indeed, one can trace the probable line of its fortifications from existing property-boundaries in the southern part of the town whose existence is recorded in the Anglo-Saxon Chronicle for the year 900.

But a study of the present town plan reveals a curious feature. Outside the irregular nucleus of the built-up area

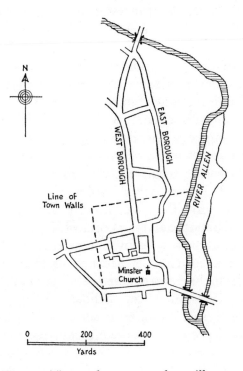

Fig. 17. The modern street plan still pre-serves the evidence for the 'new borough' added to the old Saxon town probably in the thirteenth century.

round the church, and outside the presumed line of its fortifications, are two roughly parallel streets running due north, called East and West Borough which are quite unlike the rest of the street plan. This feature is made more curious by the medieval tenurial position. The old part of the town belonged to the church of Wimborne all through the medieval period, but East and West Borough belonged to the lords of the manor of Kingston Lacey who also owned most of the surrounding rural area. Indeed East and West Borough was a separate sub-manor of Kingston Lacey with its own manorial court which continued to meet until 1880. This suggests the East and West Borough was a deliberate addition to the old town at some time. We cannot date this extension accurately, though it certainly occurred after 1086. However, from 1236 until well on into the fourteenth century there was a bitter dispute between the Church of Wimborne and the Lords of Kingston Lacey over two markets in the town of which each lord owned one and which were alleged to be 'harmful' to each other. There can be little doubt that sometime between 1100 and 1236 the Lords of Kingston Lacey deliberately created a new borough alongside the older town of Wimborne which is now indelibly preserved in the present street plan.

Ports

Except for Poole Harbour and Weymouth Bay, Dorset has a somewhat inhospitable coastline. Yet during the medieval period a line of ports grew up along it. The larger and more important ones of Poole, Wareham and Weymouth originated as deliberate plantations and are dealt with below. Further west two other ports grew up naturally in far from ideal situations, both organic developments with very different histories. *Bridport* is hardly a port at all, lying as it does one and a half miles from the coast on the tiny river

Brit. But in fact in the early medieval period small ships were able to approach to within half a mile of the town and it was able to develop as a small port, though nothing can be seen of this early harbour. The town's present wide main street is in fact its market place. The increasing size of ships later prevented them from using the river and as early as 1274 work started in making an artificial harbour at the mouth of the Brit. The subsequent history of the town is mainly the story of the continuous struggle to keep this harbour open in face of constant destruction by the sea. The harbour was rebuilt in the late fourteenth century, then destroyed and rebuilt again soon after, choked by sand in the seventeenth century, rebuilt again in 1740 and again in the early nineteenth century. But trade remained small and the coming of the railway to the town in 1857 virtually ended its life as a port. It is difficult to see in the present town and harbour this long and complex history.

Lyme Regis, in the extreme west of the county, has no natural harbour at all, and its growth from the tiny village recorded in Domesday Book to a flourishing small medieval port was entirely due to the construction of a large breakwater called the Cobb, half a mile south-west of the town. This work produced an artificial bay in which small ships could be loaded. The Cobb was probably constructed in the late thirteenth century[3] but it has been intermittently damaged by the sea and the present structure is the result of constant rebuilding from the fourteenth century onwards. As a port the town seems to have prospered only for a short while. Its fourteenth-century history is no better described than in a document of 1378 which tells us that in 1331 the town "was well built and inhabited by . . . rich and powerful merchants owning fifteen great ships and forty boats." But in 1378 the

---

[3] It is first recorded in a document of 1295 as *la Cobbe* and was possibly constructed soon after 1284 when the town was made a free borough and given a merchants' guild.

town was "for the most part destroyed and wasted by the sea and these merchants except six or eight have died or withdrawn, the Cobb . . . having been swept away last Martinmass by the sea, stopping all navigation."

Though attempts were made to revive trade, and the Cobb reconstructed, attacks by French raiders in the fifteenth century hindered the town's growth and from then until the eighteenth century it remained little more than a fishing village. Today, apart from the Cobb, there is little to see of this chequered history. The present appearance of the town, which has some of the most delightful late eighteenth-century and early nineteenth-century buildings in the county, is the result of a completely new phase of the town's history as a Regency watering place. In the late eighteenth century a Mr Thomas Hollis bought an inn and some houses in the town and persuaded Lord Chatham to visit it. It soon became a resort for fashionable Bath society, amongst whom was Jane Austen who recorded her impressions of Lyme in her novel *Persuasion*. "As there is nothing to admire in the buildings themselves, the remarkable situation of the town, the principal street hurrying into the water, the walk to the Cobb, skirting round the pleasant little bay, which in the season is animated with bathing machines and company . . . are what the stranger's eye will seek . . ."

The town prospered and grew in a small way and is still full of houses of this period which we perhaps appreciate more than Miss Austen. In the town centre are a number of attractive town houses of the late eighteenth and early nineteenth centuries, though some are in fact the fashionable refronting of older sixteenth- and seventeenth-century buildings. Most have symmetrical elevations with central doorways flanked with classical pilasters and surmounted by pediments. Some of the larger houses have fine porches supported by free-standing columns and many have delightful cast-iron balconies to their first floor windows.

Plate 36   Poole in the late eighteenth century. The town was still confined to the small peninsula on which it had been set up, with many open spaces in and around it. The long narrow lanes running between the quay and Strand Street and bounded by warehouses are clearly shown.

Plate 37 Poole today. The town has burst from the confines of the original site on the peninsula and sprawls endlessly across the once open, empty heathland

Plate 38 Dorchester, Corn Hill. Beyond the eighteenth-century town pump, the widening of South Street to become the small market place of the town can be seen.

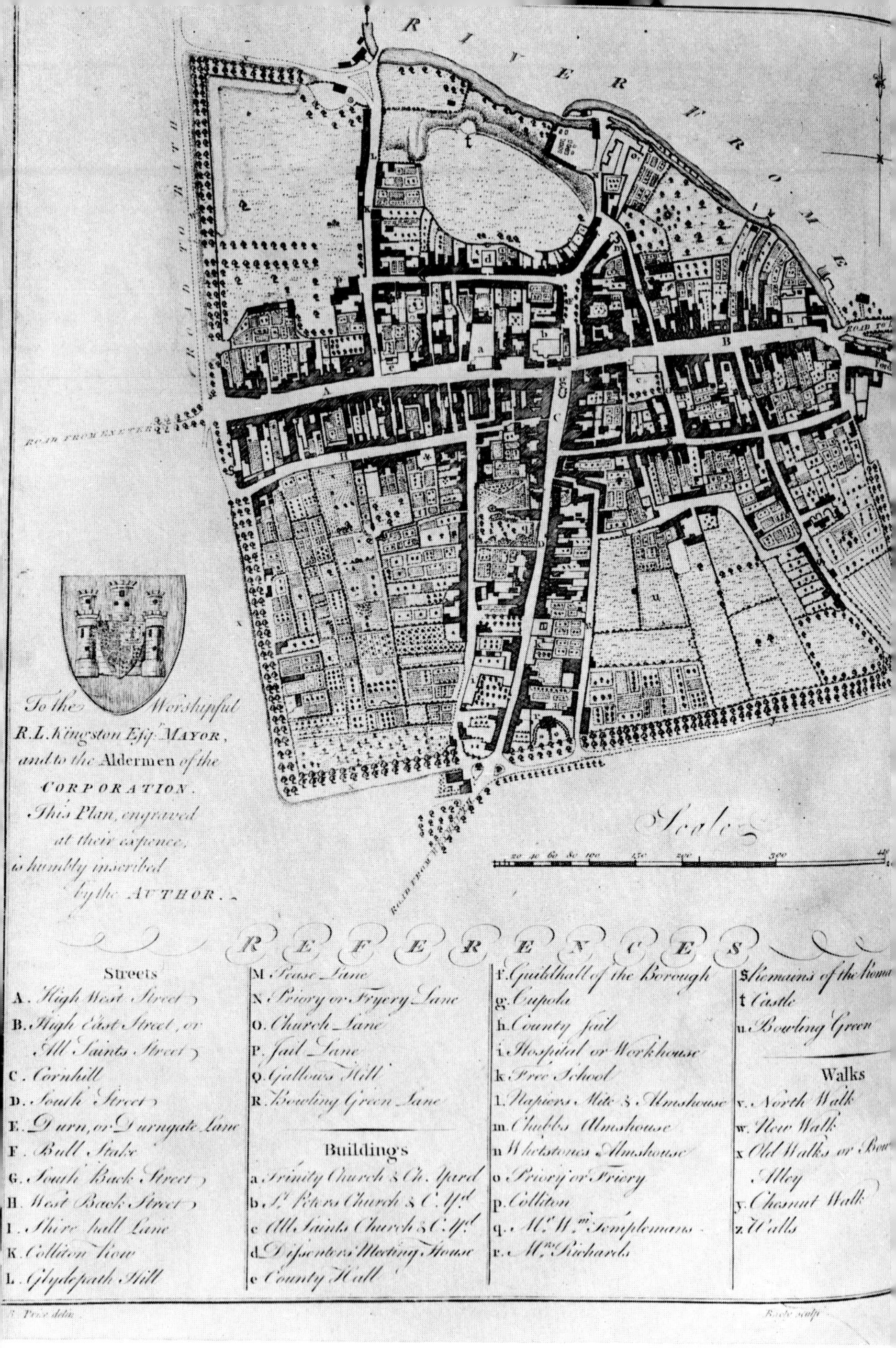
RIVER FROME
ROAD TO BRIDPORT
ROAD FROM EXETER
ROAD FROM WEYMOUTH
To the Worshipful
R.L. Kingston Esqr. MAYOR,
and to the Aldermen of the
CORPORATION.
This Plan, engraved
at their expence,
is humbly inscribed
by the AUTHOR.
Scale
20 40 60 80 100 150 200 300 410
REFERENCES
Streets
A. High West Street
B. High East Street, or All Saints Street
C. Cornhill
D. South Street
E. Durn, or Durngate Lane
F. Bull Stake
G. South Back Street
H. West Back Street
I. Shire hall Lane
K. Colliton Row
L. Glydepath Hill
M. Pease Lane
N. Priory or Fryery Lane
O. Church Lane
P. Jail Lane
Q. Gallows Hill
R. Bowling Green Lane
Buildings
a. Trinity Church & Ch. Yard
b. St. Peters Church & C. Yd.
c. All Saints Church & C. Yd.
d. Dissenters Meeting House
e. County Hall
f. Guildhall of the Borough
g. Cupola
h. County Jail
i. Hospital or Workhouse
k. Free School
l. Napiers Mite & Almshouse
m. Chubbs Almshouse
n. Whetstones Almshouse
o. Priory or Friery
p. Colliton
q. Mr. Wm. Templemans
r. Mrs. Richards
s. Remains of the Roman
t. Castle
u. Bowling Green
Walks
v. North Walk
w. New Walk
x. Old Walks or Bow Alley
y. Chesnut Walk
z. Walls
Price delin.
Basire sculp.

Plate 39 Dorchester in the late eighteenth century. The town was then still entirely within the line of the Roman walls, though these had recently been replaced by the long tree-lined Walks. It was still very small, and large areas of land within the town were not built up.

Outside the town are grander houses of the same period, set in large gardens (Plate 33). Later growth has taken the form of less distinguished architecture, but the interest and charm of its period as a watering place is still preserved.

Planned towns

As with most other English counties, Dorset has a number of towns that originated as deliberate plantations. These fall into two types, the Saxon defensive *burhs* and the later medieval commercial towns.

The Saxon burhs were conceived by King Alfred in the years preceeding the great Danish invasion of 892 and were part of a master plan whereby the whole of southern England was ringed and crossed by lines of fortresses. Some of these were short-lived due to their unsuitable position for permanent urban development. One such was *Bredie* which was placed in the west of the county to protect the area between the adjacent burhs of Exeter to the west and Wareham to the east. At this time there were no large settlements on which a new fortress could be based. On the other hand there were a number of existing fortified sites of Iron Age date in the area, and one of these was chosen for the burh. It is almost certain that the battered and mutilated hill fort known as Danes Camp or the Old Warren in Little Bredy parish was the site, standing on the crest of a high spur overlooking the Bride valley. However, though as a fortress it was well situated, its inhospitable position prevented it from developing into a town and so when the troubled times came to an end it was abandoned. Farmers in the thirteenth century, and again in the eighteenth century, ploughed over it and left traces of their plough ridges on it, and today it is hard to visualise its once vital role as a bastion of Saxon Wessex.

The burh at *Wareham* was a much more imposing fortress

and largely because of its position had a very different history (Fig. 18 and Plate 35). It was meant to protect southeast Dorset and it was built at the narrowest point of a long narrow peninsula, bounded on the north by the river Piddle and on the south by the river Frome, here less than a mile apart, at the head of Poole Harbour, a position of great tactical strength. It was not on a virgin site. Some Iron Age finds and numerous Roman finds indicate a long pre-Saxon occupation, while the Christian British inscriptions (*see* p. 46) and the burial of a king of Wessex there in 802 imply an important church or monastery which certainly existed by 876. Moreover, the place was already an important cross-channel port by the early eighth century. The existing settlement was fortified by a massive rampart and ditch enclosing some ninety acres within a rectangle of which three sides remain almost complete. A new street plan was laid out which, based on two main streets linked to four gates through the defences, produced a grid-iron pattern which still survives today. The town was thus given an opportunity for development, and its importance was enhanced in the twelfth century by the construction of a large motte and bailey castle in its south-west corner. Today this has completely disappeared except for the remains of the motte, but the line of the bailey is preserved in the present Trinity Lane which curves round the north-east side of the motte. After this early prosperity the town declined. Its trade fell away, in part due to the silting-up of the higher reaches of Poole Harbour but also because of the establishment and growth of Poole itself in a position much more suitable for trade. Wareham then became what it is today, a small market town. Its present appearance, that of an attractive Georgian town, is largely due to that curse of so many Dorset towns, fire, which in 1762 destroyed more than half of it. The rebuilding was carried out almost entirely in brick and the centre of the town remains as a pleasing group of

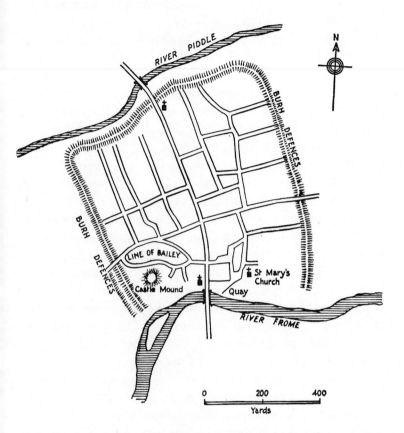

Fig. 18. On a superb site, between the Piddle and Frome, the massive defences of the Saxon burh totally enclose the town. As a result it developed the existing grid-iron pattern of streets. The tiny quay is now a quiet memorial to the once flourishing trade of early medieval times which was later taken over by the new town of Poole.

near-contemporary houses and shops. Modern 'improvements', however, have resulted in the removal of many of the best eighteenth-century doors and windows to make way for modern shop fronts.

The third burh in Dorset, *Shaftesbury*, is different again (Fig. 19). It is dramatically sited on the flat top of a spur of Greensand which projects south-west with very steep slopes 100 feet high on all but the north-east side. There is no definite evidence of earlier occupation; the burh was probably laid out on an uninhabited site. Unlike Wareham, the defences are not visible to the casual eye. The steep sides of the spur required no rampart and only a defensive wall across its neck was necessary. This still remains, very mutilated and worn, as a low rise in the ground passing through gardens and a school playground. Behind this rampart the town grew up along a single stret. Immediately outside the rampart and under its protection, King Alfred founded Shaftesbury Abbey "juxta orientalem portam Sceftisbury." It became famous with the burial there of King Edward the Martyr in 979 and grew to be the richest Benedictine nunnery in the country. This gave the new town added importance which is reflected in the existence of a small and now battered eleventh-century motte at the end of the spur. The later growth of the town is clearly to be seen in the present lay-out of its streets. The town first spread outside the confines of the fortress beyond the abbey where the existing main London–Exeter road was widened to form a triangular market place with its base against the abbey. Subsequent growth took place to the north and north-east in a relatively confined space. By the early seventeenth century, as the earliest map shows, the town was still confined to this area. The dissolution of the abbey in 1539 made little difference to the town's prosperity, though its buildings served as a vast stone quarry and were eventually reduced to the present fragments. Indeed one

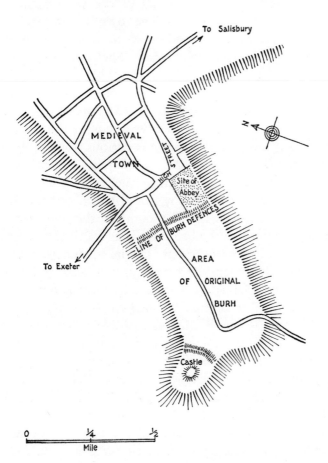

Fig. 19. The town originated as a defensive Saxon burh on a high flat-topped promontory, probably with a single central street. The establishment of the abbey on the main Salisbury-Exeter road gave the impetus for later development outside the burh. The wide High Street at the very gates of the abbey is the site of the town's market.

of the delights of Shaftesbury is the appearance of medieval carved stonework in almost all of the seventeenth- and eighteenth-century buildings. The town was in fact largely rebuilt in these centuries and no medieval secular buildings remain. As is usual in Dorset, Shaftesbury is largely eighteenth century in appearance, with some especially attractive houses of the wealthy gentry on the outskirts.

The two towns of *Weymouth* and *Melcombe Regis*, now in fact one, both originated as new towns in the thirteenth century (Fig. 20). This late date is curious, for the sites are both excellent, and one might have expected a port to have grown up there much earlier. The great anchorage of Weymouth Bay, protected by Chesil Beach and the Isle of Portland, is unique, while the mouth of the river Wey and the wide Radipole Lake behind it is an ideal situation for a harbour. The Romans certainly saw its advantages for there is evidence that they had a port at the head of Radipole Lake. But these advantages were subsequently ignored and until the thirteenth century the land on the north side of the river mouth was part of the waste of Radipole village while that on the south side belonged to Wyke Regis. Then apparently within a short time the two towns were founded, Weymouth on the south by 1244, and Melcombe on the north of the river mouth by 1268.[4] Ecclesiastically, both were served only by chapels and were dependent on the churches of their mother-villages for burials. Weymouth was laid out on a restricted site, a narrow strip of land facing its harbour, with the result that it consisted of little more than a single main street. This, though of no great signifi-

[4] There may have been small settlements on both sides at an earlier date. Melcombe is first referred to in a document of 1238, Weymouth is first mentioned by name in 1130, but one cannot be certain that this was more than the mouth of the river Wey. On the whole, the twelfth-century references seem to suggest the nucleus of a settlement. A whole string of south-western sea-ports came into existence after the marriage of Henry II with Eleanor of Aquitaine in 1152, from Poole in Dorset down to Fowey in Cornwall, the most notable perhaps being Poole, Dartmouth, and Plymouth.

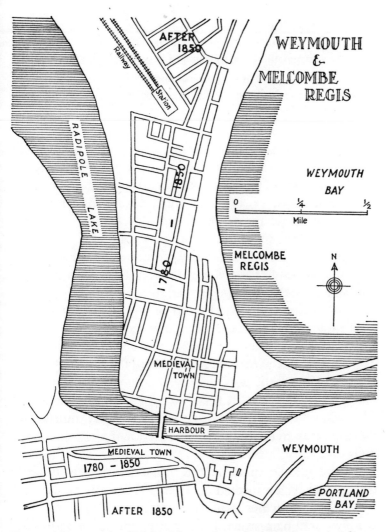

Fig. 20. The growth of Melcombe northwards along the peninsula can still be seen in the existing street plan. The grid pattern of the original medieval planned town, established in the thirteenth century, lies near the harbour. The great late eighteenth- and early nineteenth-century expansion, with its fashionable streets and terraces, lies to the north. The railway, which arrived in 1857, separates this from the more recent part of the town. Weymouth shows the same development though less clearly as a result of its constricted site.

cance during the medieval period, was to affect its later development. Melcombe was much better situated, on the southern edge of a wide stretch of land between the sea and the harbour. There was thus ample room for the town to develop. The result was that Melcombe was planned on a lavish scale, based on a regular grid of streets, which still survives almost complete in the old part of the town.

Both towns grew rapidly and by the fourteenth century were considerable ports and serious rivals for the export of wool originating from the county and beyond. In the next 100 years, however, both declined, owing in part to the growth of Poole further east, but also because of severe attacks made, on Melcombe particularly, by French raiders. In 1433 "four lakke and scarcete of helpe of peuple to withstand and resiste the malice" of the king's enemies, the port of Melcombe was closed and the wool Staple and other privileges transferred to Poole. For the next 300 years both towns appear to have been little more than small ports and probably even declined in size. Leland in the 1540s wrote of Melcombe "the towne as is evidently seene, hath beene far bigger than it is now", by which he presumably meant that part of the grid plan of streets had been abandoned. There is evidence of this in that some early nineteenth-century terraces in the old part of the town were apparently built on empty sites.

By the middle of the eighteenth century new fashions brought a change in the character of both towns. In 1748 two local gentlemen received permission to erect "two wooden bathing houses on the north side of the harbour." This was the beginning of a new prosperity. In 1780 the Duke of Gloucester spent the winter at Melcombe and the town's position as a fashionable resort was assured. By 1783 a tax of two shillings and sixpence a year was placed on every bathing machine. Soon after the Duke built himself a splendid residence, Gloucester Lodge, in a then isolated position, to the north of the town. In 1789 George III stayed at Gloucester Lodge and continued to visit the town regularly until 1811. The result was a rapid growth in both social importance and physical size. Within a short time Melcombe had outgrown its medieval confines and spread northwards along the peninsula. The present street and terrace names indicate this. The great Esplanade along the shore was started in 1785, while Gloucester Row and Royal Crescent date from the 1790s and early 1800s. The end of royal patronage after 1811 had no effect on the town's growth and indeed after that the area round Gloucester Lodge was quickly built up. Royal Terrace dates from 1816–18, Brunswick Terrace from 1823–7, Frederick Place and Waterloo Place from 1834–5 and Victoria Terrace from 1850. The architecture of all these terraces, still largely unspoilt, shows this development clearly (Plate 34). There are few places in England which show so well the rapidly changing styles and designs of upper- and middle-class urban buildings between 1780 and 1850. Individual houses and terraces all show the change from Georgian red brick and flat façades to stucco-rendered walls with at first curved bow windows and later angular bays rising through all floors or suspended at first floor level.

Weymouth, being less fashionable, did not acquire buildings of the same standard but nevertheless shared similar prosperity and growth. By the 1850s the towns were no longer in the van of fashion and building slowed down. Late nineteenth-century growth and the substantial twentieth-century expansion have done little to increase the attractive character of the towns.

Poole, too, was a medieval new town dating from around 1180, set up on a much more suitable position for trade, near the mouth of Poole Harbour, than its much older rival Wareham. It was sited on a rounded peninsula projecting into the harbour and, as at Melcombe and Weymouth, was served originally only by a chapel dependent on a rural mother-church—in this case, Canford five miles across the empty heath to the north. The street-plan of the town shows no sign of careful planning, except that the triangular market place with the town chapel, later its parish church, near its southern end seems to have been an original feature (Plate 36). The first settlement appears to have been around this market place, but subsequent development took place at the southern end of High Street and then along Strand Street. The latter is of special interest for as its name suggests it originally lay close to the water's edge. Today it is some distance from it and between the street and the present quay is a series of short lanes or alleys. These, as at Great Yarmouth in Norfolk, indicate that the shoreline has been pushed forward at some date, and records show that buildings adjacent to these lanes were always occupied by warehouses. The port grew rapidly and spread northwards to cover much of the peninsula. By the fifteenth century it had become by far the largest port between Southampton and Exeter and much of the trade of Melcombe and Weymouth was transferred to Poole. Though mainly exporting local wool, many other commodities were traded. Of this period, which was that of Poole's greatest prosperity, little remains except the street-plan. Two buildings only exist to indicate the wealth of the town at that time: the fifteenth-century Town Cellars or Wool House where wool was apparently stored, and Scaplens Court, a notable house of the late fifteenth century, once the home of a substantial merchant. The latter is an impressive building with its hall, parlour, kitchens and storehouses set round a small internal courtyard.

By the sixteenth century the town had declined as the great wool export trade fell away. Yet it soon acquired a new prosperity from a different trade which developed during the seventeenth century. This was with Newfoundland, based on imports of cod, salmon, oil, sealskins and furs. To this second period of prosperity belong the superb series of merchants' houses in the town. These are huge, double-fronted brick dwellings built by the leading merchants of the day, vying with each other in the creation of imposing residences equal to their social status. Again this prosperity came to an end in the early nineteenth century and the port was reduced to a mainly coastal trading harbour. The lack of any notable buildings of the first half of the nineteenth century reflects this.

Finally, Poole has had a third and very different period of prosperity, visually the most marked of all. By the middle of the nineteenth century that most curious phenomenon of English urban growth, Bournemouth, five miles across the heath in Hampshire had started to develop. The rapid expansion of Bournemouth has resulted in a truly enormous suburban sprawl which has engulfed the older towns of Poole and Christchurch (Hants) forming a continuous and still growing urban area. It is now fifteen miles long from east to west and nearly ten miles deep at its widest, the largest non-industrial conurbation in Britain (Plate 37). It represents perhaps the least attractive of all modern landscapes.

Three miles south of Poole, on the south side of Poole Harbour, lies *Newton*, the last of the medieval new towns of Dorset. Nothing could be in sharper contrast to Poole, for all that it is, and ever was, is a name surviving today in Newton Heath and Newton Bay. Yet its beginnings were auspicious. In January 1286, Edward I ordered that a new town be laid out here with streets, a church, building-plots, a market place and a harbour. Privileges for merchants were given and markets and a fair were granted. But nothing happened. No streets were laid out, no church built, no charter ever issued. Probably because of the proximity of the successful Poole across the water the town was never settled and the heathland remained empty. Only the names remain on maps to show that the attempt to found it was made.[5]

Resort towns

In addition to the older towns such as Poole, Weymouth and Lyme Regis which, from varied origins, have become modern resorts, the county has another, *Swanage*. Though some stone was shipped from Swanage in the medieval period, it remained little more than a fishing village until the late eighteenth century when William Morton Pitt tried to develop it into a resort on the lines of Melcombe and Lyme Regis. He converted the old manor house into a hotel which, as the Victoria Hotel, still retains a curious amalgam of two very different styles of architecture and dates. Development was slow and the town failed to become fashionable. Some indifferent houses and two early nine-teenth-century hotels remain to show this. Another attempt to raise the status of the town took place in 1825 when the present Marine Villas, near the pier, were built as Baths with a Billiard Room and Coffee Rooms above. A few pleasant terraces with stucco walls, slate roofs, and first-floor wrought-iron balconies survive from the 1830s and 1840s, but the town remained small. It gradually became a quiet, fashionable resort for professional people and in 1859 a pier was built "at which steamers touch at all states of the tide." The coming of the railway in 1881 helped and some large Victorian hotels appeared, as well as "numerous good lodging houses."[6] But it was not until this century that the town developed as a popular resort. It is now almost entirely a mid-twentieth-century and visually unattractive

[5] See Beresford and St Joseph, *Medieval England from the Air,* pp. 224–6, for a fuller account of Newton.

[6] Murray's *Handbook for Dorset* (1859 and 1899 editions).

holiday town where the observant visitor may still trace the fragments of its earlier and less prosperous phases.

Dorchester

Dorchester, the county town, takes pride of place amongst the towns of Dorset. In spite of chain-stores and other horrors inflicted on it in the name of planning, it still remains very much the Casterbridge of Thomas Hardy. In its appearance it typifies the best and worst of Dorset towns, but more important it also reflects the long, complex and continuous history of the Dorset landscape.

Its position on the south bank of the river Frome is not altogether fortuitous. Long before there was ever a town here the area was an important political and religious centre. The existence of three major sites of the Neolithic period, a causewayed camp at Maiden Castle and two so-called 'henges' at Maumbury Rings and Mount Pleasant, all close to the town, indicate the importance of the region during the third millennium B.C. The pre-eminence of the area continued for there are some 600 round barrows or burial mounds of the succeeding Bronze Age, including some of the most richly furnished in the country, within a few miles of the town. By the Iron Age not only was there a hill fort, Poundbury, overlooking the river Frome, adjacent to the present town, but at Maiden Castle stood one of the most strongly defended of all British hill forts, almost certainly the political centre of the Durotrigian tribe, and perhaps the nearest to a town that this pre-literate society could achieve.

It was to the site of the present town that the Roman army came, after subduing the Iron Age defenders of Maiden Castle, and established a fort to control the area. This fort not only gave rise to the Roman town of Dorchester but regulated its appearance and lay-out until the nineteenth century. For the outline of the fort's defences was adopted by the town to which the defeated Iron Age peoples came to learn the rudiments of Roman civilisation. Apart from one fragment of town wall and part of a house nothing remains of the Roman town *in situ*. Not even the present street-plan is the Roman one. Beyond the walls is another matter. Not only is there the amphitheatre which was in fact the converted Neolithic 'henge' of Maumbury Rings, but the fantastic aqueduct on the south side of the Frome valley which supplied the town with running water can still be traced. Even more important is the present borough boundary which swings in a wide arc west, south and east of the town. This, with some minor modifications, is the old parish boundary of Fordington, a village immediately east of Dorchester. Until the late nineteenth century the area within this boundary was occupied by the open arable fields of Fordington which extended right up to the town walls. This odd agrarian pattern suggests that this land might once have been the extra-mural territory of the Roman town itself. Though as yet there is no archaeological evidence of continuous occupation of the Roman town into the post-Roman period, the evidence of the parish boundaries implies a continuity of land-tenure which is perhaps more important.

There can be no doubt that by the early tenth century the town was a flourishing urban centre within the old Roman walls, and its importance was recognised at the Norman Conquest with the erection of a royal castle there. Of this period nothing remains standing due to constant rebuilding and in particular to the usual large-scale fires which broke out in 1613, 1622, 1713, 1725 and 1775. Nevertheless, the basic street-plan, as we see it today, must be an early feature, with two main streets meeting to form a T-shape, with the widening at the top of the upright, Corn Hill, preserving the original market place (Plate 38). This early medieval period is reflected, too, in the extremely long and narrow burgage-plots in the town centre, many of which have remained intact and controlled the form of all subsequent building.

The town was the main commercial and political centre for south Dorset during the medieval period. By the fifteenth century it was an important place for the surrounding sheep farming area and had become a textile-trading and manufacturing town. As elsewhere in the county, the wealth and prosperity that the sheep brought is reflected in contemporary ecclesiastical buildings, and St Peter's Church, one of the three medieval churches in the town shows this well. It was virtually rebuilt in the early fifteenth century, and its tower is one of the finest of this period in the county. This prosperity based on the ubiquitous sheep continued into the seventeenth century and a few surviving buildings of the late sixteenth or early seventeenth centuries help us to appreciate this. The best is that known as Judge Jeffrey's Lodgings, in High West Street, dating from the early seventeenth century. Though heavily restored, with its square-sided bay windows on the first floor and jetted top storey, it is a good example of a rich man's town house of the period.

From 1650 the textile industry declined but the town remained the centre for the surrounding agricultural region and, more important, became a fashionable place for the town houses of Dorset landowners. The town today reflects this period more than any other. The immediate impression is one of gracious, if rather provincial, Georgian houses, though these are sometimes merely façades applied to much older structures. Even by the late eighteenth century the town had not by any means filled the area within the Roman walls and there was still space for some larger town houses to be built there. Two of these, South Lodge, built in 1760, and Wollaston House in 1786, still survive. Both are small country houses in an urban setting and they indicate clearly the provincial tastes of the wealthier Dorset landowners of this period. The eighteenth century too saw the destruction of the Roman walls along the south and west sides of the town to make way for the 'Walks', exquisite tree-lined avenues along which fashionable folk perambulated. And late in the century long avenues of trees were planted along the main roads into the town. These, though partly mutilated by modern suburban growth, are still very attractive features.

Until 1850 Dorchester was Casterbridge with its assizes, its gentry, its markets and merchants. It was still totally confined within the lines of the old Roman town, and viewed from afar as Elizabeth-Jane saw it in *The Mayor of Casterbridge,* it was "an old fashioned place . . . huddled all together and . . . shut in by a square wall of trees, like a plot of garden ground by a box edging" (Plate 39). But the coming of the railway in 1847 marked the beginning of the modern expansion of the town. At first new building was still within the line of the Roman walls and some rather forbidding Victorian brick villas of the 1850s and '60s remain of this phase. But after 1874 when the open fields of Fordington finally disappeared, the suburban sprawl started in earnest. Today the street-names and the architecture still show the stages of development very clearly. Fine late Victorian middle-class villas and smaller semi-detached lower middle-class houses are carefully segregated in places such as Prince of Wales Road and Alexandra Terrace. Elsewhere the haphazard development of the late nineteenth- and early twentieth-century housing estates is clearly visible. For example, the South Court and Victoria Park estates on the south side of the town were sold for development in 1897 and the road system laid out and a few houses built immediately afterwards. But plots were sold off piecemeal in the usual fashion and it was forty years before the area was developed completely. The result is an indeterminate and unattractive sprawl so typical of English suburbia. Now the tentacles of modern development have spread even further as the town continues to extend over the fields of its Roman predecessor.

SELECT BIBLIOGRAPHY

Beresford, M. W. *History on the Ground* (1957), pp. 198–203.
Beresford, M. W. *New Towns of the Middle Ages* (1967).
Beresford, M. W. and St Joseph, J. K. S. *Medieval England from the Air* (1958).
Bowen, H. C. and Taylor, C. C. 'The Site of Newton, Studland, Dorset', *Medieval Archaeology,* Vol. 8 (1964).
Clegg, A. L. *The History of Wimborne Minster* (1960).
Fowler, J. *Medieval Sherborne* (1951).
Lloyd, D. W. 'Dorchester Buildings', *Dorset Procs.*, Vol. 89 (1958).
R.C.H.M. *Dorset, passim.*
R.C.H.M. 'Wareham West Walls', *Medieval Archaeology,* Vol. 3 (1959).
Smith, H. P. *The History of the Borough and County of Poole* (1951).
Sydenham, L. *Shaftesbury and its Abbey* (1959).
Taylor, C. C. 'Wimborne Minster', *Dorset Procs.,* Vol. 89 (1968).
Williams, G. S. 'Streets and Lanes in Wareham', *Dorset Procs.,* Vol. 64 (1943).

9. The landscape today

In spite of the great expansion of suburbia round most of the larger Dorset towns in the last 100 years, both the great beauty and the history of the Dorset landscape have been remarkably preserved for those mid-twentieth-century human beings who love and try to understand Dorset. And yet today this beauty and history are being irretrievably ruined or destroyed by what we, the same human beings, demand for the convenience of mid-twentieth-century living. The county's glorious coastline is being submerged under a sea of bungalows and caravan-parks. The vast empty heathlands are being covered by the regimented ranks of conifer plantations, ripped apart by tanks in the training areas or disfigured by atomic power stations. The grass-covered downlands have almost all gone, their hedges dating from the Saxon period to the nineteenth century bulldozed away and replaced by occasional strips of barbed wire separating acres of barley. The burial mounds, farmsteads and fields of prehistoric and Roman peoples are gradually disappearing under the plough. Some of the great country houses are derelict or have been pulled down and new road alignments to cope with the ever increasing traffic carve their way through prehistoric ditches, medieval fields and eighteenth-century parkland. This is of course not a new feature of the landscape for William Barnes, the Dorset poet, saw the same thing happening long ago:

> They do Zay that a travellen chap
> Have a-put in the newspeaper now,
> That the bit o'green ground on the knap
> Should be all a-took in vor the plough.
> He do fancy 'tis easy to show

That we can be but stunpolls at best,
Vor to leave a green spot where a flower can grow,
Or a voot-weary walker mid rest.
'Tis hedge-grubben, Thomas, an' ledge-grubben,
Never a-done
While a sov'ren mwore's to be won.

But the slow changes which Barnes noted and deplored have now reached a flood. Soon there will be little to see of the past if the present pace of change continues. Yet occasionally there is a credit side to all this in strange ways. The army, in the face of great opposition, still holds on to the west end of the Isle of Purbeck for use as a firing range. This is undoubtedly a loss to the lovers of Dorset beauty spots. But by its action, the army has preserved in the deep valley around Tyneham three virtually complete medieval field systems within the parish, and the earthwork remains of three small associated hamlets which were already old when Domesday Book was written. High on the hillside above, littered with unexploded shells, the fields cultivated by the occupiers of the adjacent Iron Age hill fort of Flowers Barrow can still be seen, while further south, similar fields have thirteenth-century plough-ridges on top of them, with traces of eighteenth-century ploughing near by. Without the army to protect them, these remains would have been ploughed to extinction years ago.

Despite all the destruction and mutilation, much of the past of Dorset survives, often in the oddest places. One can drive through the suburbs of Poole along four miles of continuous twentieth-century building to Hamworthy. Then close to the beach and set incongruously in an area of modern bungalows in Lake Road, one finds a large early eighteenth-century farmhouse, Lake Farm. It is almost the last of a group of small farms scattered along the northern edge of Poole Harbour, whose fields were hewn from the surrounding heath in remote medieval times. In fact there has been a farm on this site since at least 1327.

Or we can move north to a less populated place and climb the slopes of Penbury Knoll, a high island of downland, now lapped by a sea of arable, rising up over the north Dorset chalklands north-west of Cranborne. Looking about us on the summit we find ourselves inside an Iron Age hill fort, whose contemporary fields still impinge upon its ramparts. To the north we look across to Bokerley Dyke, one of the defences of the Britons of the fifth century. Below us to the west we can see the massive straight bank of Ackling Dyke, which is the Roman road running north to Salisbury and which cuts across a group of Bronze Age burial mounds on Oakley Down. Above on the skyline stands Wor Barrow, a Neolithic long barrow, looking down on its younger successors. Turning east we look down on Blagdon, the 'Black Down', now all arable land, but once the greatest medieval deer park in the county, covering over 1000 acres, whose park pale, a now degraded bank and ditch, actually cuts across the hill fort at our feet. But even here the twentieth century intrudes noisily upon the landscape. The roar of traffic carrying the holidaymakers to the coast wafts up to our viewpoint.

To move to a quieter place and see a marvellously preserved piece of the Dorset landscape we must journey to the north-west, and in the deep clay vale beyond Shaftesbury turn off the busy road to Exeter and start the long climb through the woods to the summit of the remarkably conical Duncliffe Hill. From the top we look south across the vale of Blackmoor and direct our gaze to the land immediately below us which is the parish of Stour Provost. Here, without even looking at a single document, we can see the whole history of its landscape preserved for us today. Over four-fifths of the parish is a well wooded heavy clay land sloping gently west with small winding streams. Beyond at the extreme west of the parish, on the edge of the river Stour which forms its western boundary, is a more open area of land on limestone. The village of Stour Provost lies on this limestone area overlooking the river. Around it on the open land we can still clearly distinguish long narrow curving fields which are the last remnants of the former open fields, now fossilised by modern hedges. The division between the limestone and the clay is visible not only because of the increasing number of trees but because of a marked change in field-shapes. Nevertheless, the field-shapes in the clay area are not all of one type. There are two very different forms. Our eyes are immediately drawn to a series of roughly circular areas, made up of highly irregularly shaped fields in the centre of which are isolated farms or small hamlets. These clearly represent the original assarts in this once forested part of the parish which were gradually enlarged as time went on and the forest slowly cut down. Even the name of one of the hamlets, Woodville, indicates its origin.

Connecting these areas of irregular fields are larger areas of more regularly shaped fields, some highly geometrical in form, which represent the later clearance of the woodlands. If we now move down the hill and wander through the parish itself we can see all these and other features even more clearly. For example, the farmsteads in the irregular field-areas are all seventeenth-century or earlier, while those in the areas of more regular fields are of eighteenth- and nineteenth-century date. If we guessed merely on shape alone that the former areas were medieval clearances and the latter were post-medieval, we should be absolutely correct. There is evidence for thirteenth-century assarting of the woodland here, as well as clearances as late as the early nineteenth century. The very lanes in the area too reflect this story. In the older cleared areas they are narrow, winding and often deeply cut into the surrounding land. In the more recently cleared places they are straight with very wide verges.

These wide verges have themselves been enclosed in many places with the establishment of a large number of eighteenth and nineteenth-century cottages of stone and brick along them. These are the dwellings of squatters or landless labourers who set up their homes here. Indeed the hamlet of Stour Row here, which is now a rival in size to the village itself, is almost entirely built on the wide verges of a straight enclosure road.

Here then, in an obscure Dorset parish, which has no great country house or specially fine church to interest us, with very few documents to unravel its story to the library-bound historian, the history of its landscape is still preserved for us to see and understand.

> Zoo now mid nwone ov us voget
> The pattern our vorefathers zet.
>
> William Barnes (*Our Fathers' Works*)

Index

Cranborne, castle, 106; Chase, 42; former market town, 174–8; House and garden, 143; medieval deer park at, 101; priory at, 83; sheep at, 90

Crawford, O. G. S., 74

Creech, Celtic place-name, 47; enclosure of heathland at, 155

Crichel House and park, 160–2

Crooked Withies, in Holt, 133

crosses, pre-conquest, 81

Damer family, 158, 160

Danes Camp, Little Bredy, 185

deer parks, 100–1, 121, 204

Dewlish, enclosure of common-fields at, 150–1

Didlington Farm, in Chalbury, 50

Digby family, 139

Doctor's Farm, in Gussage St Michael, 56

Doddings Farm, in Bere Regis, 90

Doddington, George, 142–3

Doles Ash Farm, in Piddletrenthide, 128

Domesday Book, 50, 53, 58–60, 76, 93–94, 100, 178, 180; churches in, 82; sheep listed in, 85, 89–90; use of, 84–86

Dorchester, 28; Bronze Age barrows round, 29; castle, 105, 198; churches, 82, 199; name of, 47; Roman occupation of, 33, 197–8; town of, 197–201

Drew, C. D., 54, 64

Droop, in Haselbury Bryan, 76

Druce, in Puddletown, 115

Dudsbury, hill fort, 32

Dullar, in Lytchett Matravers, 80

Duncliffe Hill, 204

Duntish, in Buckland Newton, manor of, 123; medieval deer park at, 101

Durweston, church at, 122; enclosure of downland at, 152

Earnley, in Corscombe, 101

East Bradle, in Church Knowle, 61

Eastbury House and garden, Tarrant Gunville, 142, 144

East Lulworth, sheep at, 127

East Stoke, enclosure of heathland at, 154

Edmunsham, medieval woodland in, 94–95

Edgar, king, 53

Edred, king, 50

Edwig, king, 61

Egdon Heath, 24

Egliston, North and South, in Tyneham 60

enclosures, medieval and later, 77–78, 92, 96–100, 119–20, 127–30, 205; parliamentary and private, 150–6

estates, Roman, 72–73; Saxon, 49–72

Exeter, Roman occupation of, 40

farmsteads, isolated, medieval, 63, 90–93, 96–100; deserted, 111–12

Farnham, shrunken village of, 115

fields, medieval, 77, 92, 96–100, 119–20, 205; prehistoric, 25, 27; post-medieval, 127–30, 150–6, 205; Roman, 25, 77; Saxon, 77–78

Fiddleford, in Sturminster Newton, 123

Fifehead Neville, 67

fires, in towns, 175, 178, 186, 198

Fleet, church at, 82, 163

Fleet, The, drainage attempts at, 154

Flowers Barrow, hill fort, 203

Fontmell House, in Iwerne Courtney, 142

Fontmell Magna, Saxon estate at, 49

Forde Abbey, 102, 135

forests, Bere, 92; Blackmoor, 96–98; Gillingham, 96–98

Forest Eyres, 92, 96

Fordington, 198

Forston, in Charminster, 146

Frampton, church of, 145–6; Prior of, 101; railway tunnel at, 169

Frampton, William, 154

Freke family, 145

Friar Mayne, Celtic place-name, 47; deserted village of, 113

Dorset

Frith Farm, in Stalbridge, 98
Frome Vauchurch, church at, 106
Fyloll, William, 128

gardens, 142–5, 159–62
Gillingham, 175; assarting in, 96–97; enclosure of forest in, 132; Forest, 96–97, 175; medieval deer park in, 101; textile industry in, 169
Glanvilles Wootton, enclosure of waste in, 156
Glastonbury Abbey, land in Dorset, 104; sheep on Dorset manors, 119
Godlingston, in Swanage, place-name of, 48
Grange Farm, in Holt, 94
Grange Farm, in Pulham, 98
Guest family, 159
Gummershay Farm, in Stalbridge, 98
Gummershay Farm, in Whitchurch Canonicorum, 99–100
Gussage All Saints, detached part of, 63
Gussage St Michael, Saxon estates at, 54, 56

Halstock, Roman villa and Saxon estate at, 73; Saxon charter of, 51
Hambledon, hill fort, 21, 28
Hammoon, church at, 105
Hampreston, enclosure of heathland, 154; Iron Age sites in, 32
Hamworthy, Lake Farm in, 203–4; minster parish, part of, 79
Hanford House, 138–9
Handley, 75
Harbin's Park, Tarrant Gunville, 101
Hardown Hill, Saxon burials at, 43
Hardy, Thomas, 24, 152, 197, 200
Harlyn, William, 129
Harmshay Farm, in Marshwood, 99
Haselbury Bryan, 67; enclosure of common-fields, 120; shape of village, 76
Hemsworth, East and West, in Witchampton, 75; deserted village of, 113

Henbury, in Sturminster Marshall, 80
henges, 29, 197
Henning family, 139
Hermitage, clearance of forest, 97
Hethfelton Farm, in East Stoke, 86, 92
Hewish Farm, in Milton Abbas, 116
Higher Combe Farm, in Rampisham, 147
Hilfield, enclosure of waste at, 132
hill forts, 25, 31, 169, 197, 203–4
Hilton, assarting of forest in, 97; sheep at, 127
Hinton St Mary, 67; enclosure of common-fields at, 130; Roman and Saxon estate at, 73; Roman villa at, 36, 73, 78; Saxon charter of, 51
Holt, 81; encroachments in forest at, 133–4; medieval settlements in, 94
Holwell, 67; enclosure of waste in, 155; Naish Farm in, 125
Holworth, deserted village of, 113
Honeybrook Farm, in Holt, 94
Hooke, enclosure of downland at, 128; river, 21
Horton, House, Tower and park, 161; Priory, 83; Saxon estate at, 50
Hoskins, W. G., 22, 44, 74, 93
Hurpston, in Steeple, 61
Hurst, in Moreton, 66
Hyde Farm, in Stalbridge, 98
Hyde House, in Bere Regis, 92

Ibberton, strip-lynchets at, 88
Ina, king, 46
Iron Age, hill forts, 25, 31, 169, 197, 203–4; settlements, 31, 32, 35
Iwerne Courtney, 115; church at, 145; enclosure of common-fields at, 129; Fontmell House in, 142
Iwerne Minster, 115; House and park, 162; minster church at, 78; Roman site at, 35–36
Iwerne Steepleton, 115; House, 142
Iwerne valley, deserted settlements in, 115–16; Saxon estates in, 54

Dorset

More Crichel, village and House, 160–2

Moreton, church at, 82; enclosure of heathland in, 154–5; Saxon estates in, 64–66; water meadows at, 131

Motcombe, Kings Court Palace at, 107

Mount Pleasant, Dorchester, 29, 197

Muston, in Piddlehinton, 115

Naish Farm, in Holwell, 125

Netherbury, strip-lynchets at, 99

Neolithic Period, burials, 25, 28, 197, 204; meeting places, 28, 197; settlements, 28

New Moreton, 155

Newnham, in Stalbridge, 98

'Newton', 195–6

Newtown in Witchampton, 160

Norman Conquest, place-names resulting from, 48–49

North Louvard, in Piddlehinton, 115

North Poorton, enclosure of downland at, 128

Nyland, in Kington Magna, 68

Oakley Down, barrows on, 204; medieval shepherd's hut, 90; Saxon burials at, 43

Oborne, church of, 163

Ogden Farm, in Gussage St Michael, 56

Okeford Fitzpaine, church at, 122

Orchard, East and West, in Blackmoor Vale, 67

Orchard, East and West, in Church Knowle, 61

Osmington, deserted village in, 113

Ower, 167

Owermoigne, 107

Pamphill, 81

parks, 144–5, 159–62; *see also* deer parks

Parnham House, 136, 157–8

pasture land, 89, 132, 120

Penbury Knoll, hill fort, 204

Pentridge, Celtic place-name, 47; Saxon burials near, 43

Petersham, in Holt, 94

Philliol's Farm, in Bere Regis, 92

Piddlehinton, 115

Piddletrenthide, common-fields of, 53, 151; enclosure of downland at, 128; Saxon charter of, 51–54; shape of village, 76

Pimperne, enclosure of common-fields and downland, 151–2

Pinhoe, near Exeter, 44

Pipe Rolls, 96

place-names, Celtic, 47–49; Norman, 48; medieval, 99–100; Saxon 41, planned towns, 185–96

Plush, in Piddletrenthide, Saxon charter of, 53

Poole, 193–6, 203; Harbour, 43, 148, 167–8, 182, 186, 193–5, 203

Poorton, North and South, 75, 128

population, 87, 116

Portland, 190; Castle, 148; royal manor, 106; stone quarrying at, 122, 165–6; The Verne, 163

ports, 182–5

Poundbury, hill fort, 197; railway tunnel under, 169

Povington, in Tyneham, 92

Powerstock, castle of, 105; church at, 105; strip-lynchets at, 99

Poxwell House, 139–40

Poynington, church at, 105

Preston, in Iwerne Minster, 115

Puddletown, Bardolfston in, 108; church at, 82, 123; deserted settlements in, 115; sheep at, 90; turnpike road at, 171–2; water-meadows at, 131

Pulham, East and West, 68; enclosure of waste at, 133; medieval settlements in, 98, 133

Pulston, in Charminster, 138

Puncknowle, Manor House and gardens, 143

Purbeck, 22, 27, 203; Iron Age occupation in, 32, 35; limestone, 165–7; marble, 165–7; quarrying,

212